DiOrio, Ralph A.
The Healing Power of
Affirmation

DATE DUE			

The Healing Power of Affirmation

The Healing Power of Affirmation

Fr. Ralph A. DiOrio

Doubleday & Company, Inc.
Garden City, New York
1985

Most scriptural citations are from *The Jerusalem Bible* Copyright ©
1966 by Darton, Longman & Todd, Ltd. and Doubleday & Company,
Inc.

Library of Congress Cataloging in Publication Data

DiOrio, Ralph A., 1930–
    The healing power of affirmation.

    1. Christian life—Catholic authors.   I. Title.
BX2350.2.D54   1985   248.4'82   84–25903
ISBN: 0-385-18227-9

Frontispiece drawing by Mona Mark

Contents

LORD, THE ROAD CAN SHOW ME MANY THINGS

Lord, the road can show me many things.
It has an end. There is no road without an end.

   Its purpose is to lead me to the end,
My life too has an end and purpose: glory with the Father!
The way leads over mountains, and through vallies.

   Nothing can stop it. It leads over the obstacles.
Let me not, O Lord, yield to obstacles, and let me courageously
overcome all difficulties.

   The road is silent; how many sufferings it unveils
along its long journey! How many secrets are entrusted to it.
   But it does not betray them to the traveler.
Teach me the art of silence, O Lord!
   The road is there for all men: for the luxurious car,
for the farmer's cart, for the worker going to the factory,
and the farmer driving to his field; for the schoolboy
     and the mailman,
for the priest who brings you to the sick, for one and all.

   Lord, I would also like to be there for all men.
Grant me a ready heart. Let it be my joy to serve
all men according to your example.

Lord, the road can show me many things. You have already said

I AM THE WAY!

AUTHOR UNKNOWN

Preface

To wander no more is an aspiration of every pilgrim. To be a wanderer is to move without an apparent definite purpose or objective. The wanderer is a man or a woman, a young or older adolescent, a boy or a girl—anyone who is confronted with the awesome reality that *to discover the world can be very painful.* The wanderer is any human person, regardless of race, nationality, or creed. Better still, the wanderer is a *pilgrim:* a wayfarer, a sojourner, a traveler on a journey. He or she—whoever and whatever the situation or the case may be—is on a journey of discovery. To be a wanderer does not mean that one is lost; it only points out that one is searching.

Does the true wanderer—while in search—not know that he or she is trying desperately hard to bring forth into fruition what God the Creator put into human hearts? The wandering pilgrim seeks and searches down the labyrinthine ways of his or her mind, down the arches of the years—searching, searching for that one sound, that one place where he or she really fits. The search goes on for years. It is often a reckless hunting to find some people with whom to identify, something with which to harmonize. And as we continue throughout the years of life, we continue on struggling from place to place, wandering as it were. But with each wandering step we recognize more closely the eternal truth that God put something inside of us. We can shout joyfully, "Yes, I am wandering, I am in search, I am a pilgrim; but when I find it, I'll know what it's like!"

The beauty of wandering is that for many it is a natural process allowed by the Creator; and without it, one may never become what the Creator meant one to be. God plants something very special in each human being. But circumstances and conditions, persons and places that are unforeseen and even unwanted can come across our paths. These experiences in turn stifle, confuse, and perplex a person. And each man's wandering journey will bring him into a number of experiences: some good, others not. But the beauty of it all is the discovery that there is *more* to the quest than that particular momentary experience.

Amusing as it may be, such a wandering is illustrated in this story many of us evangelists tell. There was a handsome man who was drafted into the Army. And every day as he walked along he kept picking up pieces of paper, saying to himself but audibly, "That's not it!" He would pick up one piece after another and say, *"That's* not it! *That's* not it; *that's* not it!" He went on doing this for about six months. And so his superiors became concerned. They brought him into a special, nicely decorated room: the psychiatrist's office. And the doctors said to him, "What's wrong with you? What's your problem?" And the man answered, "I don't know. What do you mean what's my problem?" The doctors said, "Well, there's got to be something wrong with you because you keep going all over this base, picking up small pieces of paper, saying 'that's not it, that's not it.' Now, just WHAT are you LOOKING for?" The man repeated, "I don't know! But I do know that I just don't seem to be able to find it." Well, the doctors and the officials conferred, and they said to him, "We think your problem is serious; and we're going to give you a medical discharge from the service." And when they handed the discharge paper to him, the man excitedly shouted out, *"THIS* IS IT!"

Now, if you have been a wanderer going about looking for IT, if you are diligent in your searching, if you can distill from your mind and life the kinds of things you have allowed to make you a stranger to the blessings of God, you will eventually conclude your journey of wandering. Your pilgrimage will be the discovery of who you are, who your God is; and when you come to this smashing knowledge, you will possess the power of knowing where you are going! Every pilgrim in search of meaning eventually comes to the joyful realization that the greatest gift a human being can receive is a deeper understanding of life and the ability to love and believe in self.

Each of us has a path to travel. *Like the experience of death, life, once lived, is like a PATHWAY of NO RETURN.* Indeed, life is a pathway; and once we have traversed it, there is no possible means of going back. We shall not pass this way again; and that reality should encourage the wanderer in us. It should echo and reecho in our minds.

To wander no more is truly a noble aspiration just as to heal and to build is a noble task. With each age, amid human and social perplexities, there still comes across the land a rainbow of hope for a better tomorrow through the honest, sincere emergence of "the Self." Within every human being there resides a restlessness, the volcanic bubbling that the best of YOU is yet to be. Let this book and my reflections be a voyage within for you—a voyage of reflection, deliberation, and decision. Perhaps for some it will influence and inspire into action: the response/action of *recogniz-*

ing yourselves, *repenting* your errancies, and *rededicating* your whole person afresh with a New Baptism of the power of the Holy Spirit.

Every human person, in the beauty of his or her own self, is definitely and decisively "called" *not* simply to "achieve," but rather to "be." The contents of this book endeavor to bring each human soul into a self-encounter of personal evaluation. As these chapters lead you into the evaluation of the various phases of living, it is hoped that the virtue of honesty to self will surrender itself to the power and the strength of humility. That humility reflected in the "holy presence" of the Creator will offer the spark of revival, renewal. The topics here do not pretend to be comprehensive or all-inclusive. But, selective as they are, I hope you find them determinative and enriching and encouraging.

Truth will be confronted in these pages; but there will remain no place for discouragement, despondency, or despair. As long as we are on this side of eternity, hope is always available to us. I will deal with basic elements and situations which are universally felt by all peoples. Life in all its "livings" is a Broadway with many side streets. None of us can escape this human business of living, of playing one's part in the *struggle of surviving*. These universal experiences will never exempt a man or a woman, an adolescent or a child; even the aged are no strangers to them.

Life has its own particular way of leading a human voyager. Sometimes life pilots a person up to the lofty heights of the mountains, at other times into the dark and bleakness of the valleys. There are many moments when life brings tears and harsh experiences. Our pain is deep as it is intensely real. Our dreams and lofty aspirations are counteracted by such agents as obstinacy, sloth, doubt, fear, presumption. Others, as deceptive as these, make their cunning entrance: hypocrisy and worldliness, passion in all its forms. But the Pilgrim Traveler does not need to crawl in the valleys of destruction. From the brokenness of his or her humanity, the traveler needs only to look up beyond the clouds and see the Lord of all Creation, beg the Lord's presence, and with renewed strength conquer the capturing giant of despair. The result: a soul regenerated, renewed, revitalized to fly aloft again on eagle's wings.

Many persons—too many indeed—surrender to hopelessness. If one who is stripped of everything cannot commit suicide, he or she necessarily seeks a "filling up." That which is empty of God will of its own seek to fill itself with the human—if not the less than human. One danger of emptiness is that it makes one ready for a love affair—an affair of love —but not love in itself. Emptiness prepares a discouraged human voyager for a "filling up" with all forms of escapism. Some of these are definitely neurotic; many others are make-believe, substitutions for reality. The human mind is so tricky in its defenses—and do you blame it? It is seeking self-survival. Pain, however, is the result; and *that* can be bad!

The destruction of the self through filling up with wrong decisions and irrational behavior says that the person considers himself "inadequate." This thinking, especially if translated into action, will be destructive. Hopelessness eventually will lead to despair. Without FAITH there can be no hope.

Perhaps it is faith that will save this human brokenness. Perhaps it is faith not in our human contrivances, human strengths, but a faith in HIM, the Creator of heaven and earth, Author of life, and Governor of all existence. Perhaps when a human pilgrim can meet his God this way he can come to realize that "the best is yet to be."

These topics of reflection have their own dynamics; they are personal to each reader; but at the same time they are applicable to situations affecting the universal human condition. The sinner of the moment can be the saint of the next. Fear disappears in the grace of the Almighty; and the journey within oneself becomes a joyous discovery of the real self— *you.* What freedom that produces: to become FREE as God created and meant you to be!

This journey will not offer a mask, a false "persona." It will not conceal our humanity with its rights and its duties, its privileges, even its responsibilities. This book will offer to the crying honest heart a tranquil investigation into our human nature's weaknesses and its powers for restored beauty and affirmation. We go within to the very core, the very nerve of human sensitivity. Divine Grace will fall upon—and only upon —the humble human soul. Divine Grace will reveal TRUTH. Divine Grace will beckon forth both the human and the spiritual realities; WHO we are, WHO our God is, WHERE we are going.

When we look and focus on the Divine Power, then every happening in our lives suddenly makes sense. Both the GOOD and the BAD events fit together like pieces of a mosaic forming, as it were, a total image of who each person *is*—in himself and before his God.

The "soul in journey" will herein see the excellence of values. I ask that you read and meditate in prayerful reflection and deliberation. Do not read these thoughts primarily to seek information; but read that you may render your goal about living wisely. There is a power all and exclusively its own—deeply inherent to spiritual reading. This power decreases our natural instincts; and as it empties us of ourselves, it allows Him to enter, filling us with His refreshing love. Such an approach to reading increases within us a docile spirit for resurrected faith, restored hope, and the new birth. It renders us obedient and submissive to His plans for each of us. It inspires us personally to muster a change of heart.

Above all, it is this writer's prayer and hope, as it is his joy, to share with you the very best of heaven and earth. It is good to be broken, it is good to have made a mistake, because without that mistake our brokenness would not have left us empty to receive HIM who gives us HOPE.

PART I
Values

1.

To Be or Not to Be

I will never forget you.
See, I have branded you on the palms of my hand,
your ramparts are always under my eye.

ISAIAH 49:15–16

The greatest tragedy in life is a human person who dies inside while he lives. In moments of despair such dying is very easy, and it comes very quickly. It is atrocious in its onslaught. One who loses all trust in the elements of earth may still look upward for that one last hope; and in that one last dying gasp for survival, one cries out to SOME INVISIBLE POWER, some invisible force that will tell him who he is, what life is *really* all about, whether there is anything *real* outside this existence. Such a woeful cry from such a destitute soul evokes these sensitive words of Mary Dixon Thayer:

Who am I, Lord, who dare to pray?
And yet—ah, do not turn away!
Such as I am, I come to Thee, such
as I am, Lord, pity me. Accept
the will that is so weak, the love
I know not how to speak. The
Little broken offering of all I am.

A PRAYER

Tragedy is an evil thing. And though God cannot will evil, He can nevertheless utilize it for a higher beneficial purpose. Like an artist using the chisel, He can use a supposedly evil catastrophe in the sculpturing of our character. Tragedy has a power to bring people together. People are at their best when they are running to the aid of another human in need, giving the best of self to the other. And the greatest gift to another human person is the very gift of oneself in the true, unselfish bond of supportive friendship.

This fraternal interaction of concern and of self-giving can reveal a great deal. People, by nature, are often afraid to interact on a personal basis. They fear that by so doing they will disclose their inner secrets. The fear is not the disclosure; but the fear is that through disclosure the other party may become disappointed and reject them. This is tragic. It is unbearable.

On the other hand, when we offer assistance, a beautiful and positive insight is revealed. This type of disclosure comes in many forms: for example, when we find the right person to love or when we witness the mystery of childbirth or when we relocate in a new town, city, or country to start a new life. Again, it may come during or after a period of depression, or at the time when we seem to be going nowhere.

What the above reflects is that God is always on the move, always trying to form a people unto Himself, trying to call into harmony those who are wandering, searching. And though we seem to be going nowhere, God is mysteriously moving us. He is making Himself available to be known, loved, served, and to become the ultimate reward for everyone who knows that he or she is "chosen" to become part of that which is great.

God is always revealing His Presence to us, in every circumstance, in every experience of our humanity. His voice thunders with His esteem for us: "You are a chosen people; you are a holy nation; you are part of a royal priesthood; you have been called out of darkness, out of your wandering. You are being summoned unto a marvelous life to share the glories of Him who calls you." And so He tells us: "Hang on awhile; wait it out. Don't abandon. There is a rainbow of hope that is sweeping over the land; and its blessings are falling upon everyone in the land who is willing to *recognize, repent, and rededicate.*"

So, then, though tragedy may have its impact, no tragedy has the power to destroy unless we believe it can, unless we ourselves allow it to hurt us. Everyone can build on ruins. To heal and to build is a noble task.

To exemplify this point, allow me to recount a tragedy that taught one of America's most loved comedians, Lou Costello, a way to happiness. Mr. Costello related this episode to his dear friend Vivian Cosby. Lou was stricken with rheumatic fever. As he lay in bed week after week, he kept asking himself, "Why did this have to happen to me?" And what had made this illness all the more bewildering was that Lou Costello had become ill while on a tour to raise funds for charity, while striving to help others. The question "Why?" plagued him incessantly. The more he thought about it, the sorrier he felt for himself. Very often Lou would torment his mind as he reflected on the seven years of hard struggle that it had taken him and Bud Abbott to achieve success. Now in his moment of weakness and brokenness, he anguished over whether he would ever perform again. Very frequently his family would observe him in solitude, crying over "the guy named Lou Costello."

So with Lou Costello, well loved by millions of people, the grace of the moment, God's unseen healing touch, would tap a dormant reservoir of spiritual power. That incident of utter distress suddenly sparked a resurrection of new hope. Lou recounts that one morning when his wife, Ann, brought in his breakfast tray and the morning paper, the paper was folded over to a story about a little girl named Goldie. The doctors had given this child only six months to live. Here was a child doomed to die, even before she had really started life. The story bothered him; Goldie was on his mind the rest of the day. Finally he telephoned his doctor to ask him to look into the case. The doctor's findings resulted in Lou Costello sending the little girl to the Mayo Clinic. Eventually, little Goldie was cured.

Many people came to Lou to thank him for helping Goldie. Then suddenly, out of the depths of his inner humanity, came forth the healing medicine for Lou Costello himself. He heard himself reply, *"I AM GRATEFUL, VERY GRATEFUL THAT I HAD THE MONEY TO DO IT."* It was the word "grateful" that offered Lou Costello the prescription for sorrow: "COUNT YOUR BLESSINGS." And so he began to count his; and the more he did, the more the reality impressed him that God's blessings to him outnumbered his misfortunes.

The grace of God will bestow itself in moments least expected. God utilizes strange ways through which He speaks to us. That which will keep men and women alive is honor. A life with honor sometimes exposes one's human inadequacies. These are replenished and vitalized by Him who created each one of us *with purpose.* No matter how trying and destitute our lives become, the affirmation of God's presence beside us brings each one of us to the stark reality that THERE IS NO LOST ADVENTURE! The adventure of human nature is a quest for happiness. As George Jacques Danton proclaimed, just prior to ascending to the guillotine, "[To conquer] we have need to dare, to dare again, ever to dare!"

Probably sometime or other we all have experienced some great insight. When it does come, it hits us hard, but with clarity. It is usually a "new awareness," an awareness of our human nature that helps us to grow, especially spiritually. Escape is never the answer to problems or questions. The wonder of escape leads only to further befogging.

On the other hand, how much more consoling is the thought that we need never escape our human existence. Strange as it may seem, nevertheless, it is a reality that the very solutions to our human conditions *dwell right inside,* within us. They are closer than we realize. If we would take this voyage of discovery into ourselves, surrendering our fears in life to the Almighty God's promising grace, then mental, psychological, and spiritual healing will inevitably ensue. Such an awareness furnishes *meaning* and *direction.* Without it, every one of us may as well set sail on a futile, frivolous ocean voyage of no discovery, of no return. We would be exactly as a ship without a compass. With meaning, however, there is the possibility of fostering authentic revived strength. This is the key to victory over the challenges in life.

A few months back a national TV station aired a rerun of a science fiction film. The movie depicted a selected group of scientists, whose goal was to enter into the human body and to detect the unknown cause of sickness afflicting an ill person. The scientists were placed in a submarine. The submarine was scientifically reduced in size; and both the scientists and the submarine were then injected into the veins of a sick person. The journey within that system began; they traveled through the body, organ by organ was observed, each sound and palpitation of the living organs monitored. They observed, ascertained, discovered the causes of the disorder. In the course of the journey, however, the great discovery was that each scientist found God, as they found a Living Soul within the person.

Fantastic? Maybe so. But great instances of insight transform us; and if we are unprejudiced, they can occasionally transfigure the dregs of personal lives as well as those of society on the whole. Whatever the source of insight, be it an incident or an accident, be it a blessing or an apparent curse, be it our emotions of love or hate, sadness or joy, pleasure or pain, despair or boldness, be it a volcanic bubbling of anger—from all of these, vented positively or negatively, God can offer insight into His plan for you and me, all of us.

Each of us—everyone—has a definite, distinctive place in God's blueprint. God certainly cannot will evil; but on the other hand, He is willing not to be outdone in His wisdom. He knows how to transform tragedy into victory.

What man permits, God will purify. God's permissive media for insight can serve as an important link in our growth and human pilgrimage to Him. God is able to speak to us, for example, through the innocent eyes of a child, the fading away of an evening sunset; through the many splendors of nature in all its portrayals of the Creator: the rose in bloom, the majesty of lofty mountainous heights, the onrushing power of rivers and falls. All of creation is an encyclopedia of God speaking to man. What a revelation of truth!

The human spirit is often compared to a hiker trekking through the forest on a pleasant spring day. All about him abound the flourishing unfoldings of Mother Nature in her virginal best. Nevertheless, amid this very beauty there is restlessness, struggle, and bewilderment. There are so many trees in the darkened forest, and the path often forks into many directions. We get no clear idea of what exists beyond the forest. But then, all of a sudden, from above the very trees that seemed before to offer only darkness, there beams a bright ray of light. It points to a clearing. The forest ends, and he who ventured a journey of discovery as a hiker now safely arrives to where he has ventured: a scene of tremendous natural beauty. He has dared to dare; he has borne his human nature through thick and thin to the reality that no adventure is lost. He sees where he has come from and where he must continue to tread. The goal and the affirmation of someone's presence has made the day's hiking worthwhile.

Most of us go through life knowing only half of ourselves. For this reason, many of us use only half of our resources, a meager amount of our abilities. We surrender confidence to skepticism, timidity, self-doubt, and ultimately, to irresolution. The way to happiness is lost through the lack of confidence. Despair is just around the corner. The mind temporarily dwells on the street of dispiritedness with its adjacent neighbors of depression, anger, and lack of self-contentment. And in this emotional waste, this mental anguish and physical breakdown, great areas of hidden strength remain dormant. We truly suffer because we are strangers to ourselves. Healing prayer is jeopardized as it providentially attempts to revive the human soul to stand at its full stature as initially planned by God. Holistic restoration is blocked by a thousand and one *escapisms,* be they neurotic exaggerations of "ego defense" or psychotic substitutions of a make-believe world for the world of responsibilities by which we all must live. One's irrational use of fear spurns the healthy self-appraisal questions that must be asked: (1) What sort of person am I? (2) What do I think about and why do I behave as I do? (3) What are my blind spots, weaknesses, my special personality shortcomings that I either fail to recognize or refuse to acknowledge? (4) How do emotional frustrations affect my everyday behavior? (5) Have life's confrontations distorted my sense of values? (6) Am I immature in my development of character, in my attitude toward love, sexuality, people, life in general? (7) What subconscious motivations wrestle and agitate within me, producing both prejudices and hatred? (8) Am I behaving like a little boy or a little girl in an adult body, too egocentric, too oversensitive? (9) Do my own inadequacies, my own failures seek the scapegoat, the blaming of others for my own failures? (10) As I approach my present goal in this mundane, material life, do I ignore the ultimate goal of eternal life: to grow, improve, and to be what God meant me to be?

The *awareness* of being broken is the first step to bringing tranquillity as well as renewed endeavor into our handling of personal and interpersonal difficulties. A short time each day devoted to analyzing our faults and weaknesses will enable us to muster appropriate corrections. A bit of honest day-to-day self-knowledge, self-discipline, and determination to acquire a new set of thinking habits will render the opportunity of giving birth to what the Scriptures describe as "THE NEW MAN INVESTED IN JUSTICE AND TRUTH."

Herein lies the point of our interest; herein emerges the theme of our book. Namely, God taking our broken humanity in all its guises, accepting each one of us exactly as we have made ourselves, embracing you and me, purifying each of us in the alchemy of His sacred heart, washed clean in His precious blood, and sent forth to witness to other human beings the unchangeable message *I have carved you in the palm of My hand. You are precious to Me, I have called you by name.*

The new man clothed in truth and justice is he who has faced reality. Truth and reality compel an honest person to continuously evaluate priorities. Such areas considered objectively are the maxims and affections of the world. The divinely graced soul, renewed and revitalized in the vista of godliness, humbly entreats the Lord to divest it of the old man with his former, unworthy thoughts and conduct. In both Ephesians 4:24 and Colossians 3:10, St. Paul emphasizes this clothing of the new man according to the Lord. You must give up your old way of life; you must put aside your old self, which gets corrupted by following illusory desires. Your mind must be renewed by a spiritual revolution so that you can put on the new self that has been created in God's way, in the goodness and holiness of truth. That is why you must kill everything in you that belongs only to earthly life: fornication, impurity, guilty passion, evil desires, and especially greed, which is the same thing as worshiping a false god; all this is the sort of behavior that makes God angry. And it is the way in which you used to live when you were surrounded by people doing the same thing, but now you, of all people, must give all these things up: getting angry, being bad-tempered, having spitefulness, using abusive language and dirty talk, and telling each other lies. *You have stripped off your old behavior with your old self, and you have put on a new self which will progress toward true knowledge the more it is renewed in the image of its creator.*

It is a basic tenet of psychology and ethics that none of us can live life without a sense of our own worth. One can easily see, therefore, that self-knowledge is the ultimate victory. Self-knowledge itself begets the gentle virtue of humility. Before this virtue of truth as to who or what someone is, the quality or condition of being arrogant no longer lends itself as a means to conceal shortcomings, but renders itself to the victorious joy of self-conquest.

The great tragedy of life is to have God, our Creator, within our beings, or about us through the various forms of His creation, and not to give birth to His mysterious Divine Architect's plan. The foolish reaction to life's situations and problems is to choose and adhere to all that excludes the mind of God which made all things to converge. Yes, to bring into oneness every little thing in the universe, from a glittering snowflake composed of all its crystal accumulations to the dispirited or forsaken prisoner in confinement.

Meeting God, meeting His Divine Son, walking in the conviction of the Holy Spirit of truth means coming into contact with the ultimate reality. In the light of reality illusion with all its false perception melts away. Meeting God is meeting Truth. Meeting God in Truth disintegrates illusion. It exposes escapism as cowardice. There can never be any peace until there is "inscape." Each of us experiences a cry to be born.

But exactly what is this cry dwelling within that wants "to be born"? It is that inscape that reveals the meaning and the goal of life through a spiritual, moral, and mental security. It is law, order, rhythm, pattern, purpose. Both the ancients and the modern thinkers have identified it as a philosophy of life. It delves into the mystery of God; and God in turn makes the searcher of truth intelligible, and He gives life a meaning. But the greatest impression of the "voyage within" is finding a refuge in the Almighty God of Love. The beauty of it all is that the voyage does not halt in internal revelation and the sense of security; inscape does not serve solely for a flight from reality. There must be a return to reality, to life with all its responsibilities.

Another enriching result of meeting God through inscape is that though our illusions are destroyed, we are not left crushed. His presence is active; it is alive! Our "inner journey" with God leaves us with an altogether different basis for *confidence*. This confidence is Christ Jesus, our Blessed Lord. Paul, speaking to the Philippians (4:19), stated this point: "In return my God will fulfill all your needs, in Christ Jesus, as lavishly as only God can." And again Paul encourages us when, in 1 Thessalonians 5:9, 10, he utters: "God never meant us to experience the Retribution, but to win salvation through our Lord Jesus Christ, who died for us so that, alive or dead, we should still live united to Him."

Jesus is always victorious. If we establish our relationship with Him, we shall see His power demonstrated in our lives, our hearts, our service and interactions with people. To be broken is painful; it is humiliating; but it is the only way that we with St. Paul can joyously attest: "I have been crucified with Christ, and I live now not with my own life but with the life of Christ who lives in me. The life I live in this body I live in faith; faith in the Son of God who loved me and who sacrificed Himself for my sake." (Gal. 2:20)

Our Blessed Lord wants to reveal Himself. He wants union with us through the bond of love. He does this with His resurrection power. But He can accomplish our salvation directly only through our own brokenness, that is, death to self, death to our attitudes. Jesus knew human nature. He understood the fickleness, the instability of the heart of man. He knew so well that like Simon Peter a man can be swept away in a moment of emotion, and then back out when he discovers what his decision really implies.

Meeting Our Blessed Lord, the Son of God, reveals the Trinity, Father, Son, and Holy Spirit, at work in us. He works in us as an all-encompassing merciful God continuously unveiling Himself through religion. And with this force God shows how religion can be part of our self-image. He allows us to experience religion as something we may build into our lives to provide ourselves with respectability. This very God-gift, religion, can further offer itself as a meeting with the living Christ who takes us and reveals to us a way that is not of our own making. And therefore, to share in Christ's life, we must be willing to participate in His suffering and death, in the suffering and death of our humanity whose arms are frantically outstretched and reaching for His resurrection and our hope.

God cloaks our sins; God binds our wounds. He does all this because He unconditionally loves you; He loves me. Jeremiah (18:1–12) so nicely states the excellence of restoration when he picturesquely describes the potter and the clay. In essence, the human soul depicted by the clay can only humbly but joyfully pray: "You lifted me out of the pit, you found me. O Lord, you reached down and found me, you picked me out distinctively, out of my old life."

Ezekiel, furthermore, consoles mankind in his words: "I myself will pasture my sheep, I myself will show them where to rest. It is the Lord Yahweh who speaks. I shall look for the lost one, bring back the stray, bandage the wounded, and make the weak strong; the sick I will heal, shepherding them rightly." (Ezek. 34:15,16)

As you make this journey within, you might become frightened. You may appear—but only appear—to lack courage to rise again. But arise you must; we must! Let not your wounds—no matter what they are, even if they be as crimson red—surrender you to discouragement. Do not allow your dispirited soul to turn miserably from the Heavenly Embrace. Instead, believe and trust in God's fatherly love, understanding, and mercy. Instead, let those very wounds that led away from the Lord become the very steps to the Divine Physician's healing remedy. Our wounds need tending; allow the Divine Physician to commune. Speak not much. But in humility, produced by the reality of our weaknesses, just timidly though confidently, submit to the Master. Speak not much; but listen. Move not; but rest. Then the Father will make Himself visible to your faith, to your hope, to your love by healing you with the presence of His Divine Son.

This union with God, this closeness to Him cannot come about overnight. It is not of our making. Our sins and transgressions are of our human making. But if we ask Our Blessed Lord to come and live within us, then He will transform you and me by His spirit.

Recently, a teenager going through a time of search for meaning and for *someone constant* was suddenly overwhelmed by Divine Grace. The teenager's soul was transformed by God's presence in His Holy Word. The teenager was reading John 14:1–3: "Do not let your hearts be troubled. Have faith in God and faith in me. In my father's house there are many dwelling places: otherwise, how could I have told you that I was going to prepare a place for you? I am indeed going to prepare a place for you, and then I shall come back to take you with me, that where I am you also may be." *(NAB)*

We received this written attestation from the teenager:

Those were very difficult years for me. Deep in my heart and soul I felt a battle going on within me. I was not sure what to believe. My parents were good parents, but faith and the church did not have priority. It was in my last two years of high school that I found myself in a spiritual struggle. The religious truths I was reading and studying in school were making a lasting impression on me. I could not get enough knowledge about Jesus. The words in the old Baltimore Catechism became embedded in my mind. "God made me to know Him, to love Him, and to serve Him in this world so that I may be happy with Him in the next." To me this meant only one thing. In my young mind and heart I felt the only way to fulfill this to the best of my ability was to leave the world behind me and try to learn more about God so that I might love Him more and then be able to help my family and others come to love Him also.

Then I came to understand that I could still be a part of the world and love God. I did not have to flee the world. In loving others I was not loving Him less. Jesus' words began to make sense to me. "I DO NOT ASK YOU TO TAKE THEM OUT OF THE WORLD, BUT TO GUARD THEM FROM THE EVIL ONE." (John 17:15)

2.

Quest for Happiness

*Something hidden. Go and find it. Go and
look behind the Ranges—
Something lost behind the Ranges. Lost and
waiting for you. Go!*

KIPLING, "The Explorer"

It's an important thing to stay alive; so try to live exactly the life you really were meant to conduct happily. It's a good thing to live concernedly for others; but it's necessary to live concernedly for yourself, too. Appropriate living first experienced within oneself eventually overflows into appropriate sharing with other human beings. In this healthy sequence of events one will find oneself on the way to happiness.

Our search for truth and love, beauty and perfection, indicates that something is lacking in us for the fullness of life. The yearning for happiness is related to the noble passion of hope which, in its simplest form, is a gaze toward the future. The goal of life must satisfy the highest reaches of personality, namely, our desire for life, our craving for truth, and our holy passion for pure love. Our wills are not satisfied merely by a love that grows cold or has phases like the moon, but by a love that is a continuous ecstasy without any feeling of hate or satiety. This perfect life, this perfect truth, this perfect love is God: Father, Son, and Holy Spirit.

God is always speaking to us through a thousand different ways. He is constantly unfolding and demonstrating His love for us. In His love alone, recognized in all things, dwells the fullness of happiness. The great "miracle of happiness" is to know the moment when it happens. Why is this? The reason rests in the actuality that man's search for happiness is man's search for adequate fulfillment. Moreover, a man's happiness does not consist in the abundance of things he possesses. Regardless of how much we possess or acquire, life on earth for all of us is at one time or another impinged on, if not totally shocked, by evil, miseries, and sufferings. Failure in the quest of happiness brings about a series of disappointments, traumas, and disillusionments. One thereupon reacts either cynically or religiously.

Is there any solution at all, therefore, to all this "valley of tears"? If one instinctively craves and wants happiness, one then must have been created for it. If one is disappointed here, it must indicate that that person is seeking happiness in the wrong places. Logically, therefore, he or she must conclude that it is to be found somewhere else. And that is God. In every person's life span there are interludes of unquenchable happiness. Yet, like the flickering of a sunbeam, like a fleeting, caressing breeze, these are only dim shadows of the eternal and incomprehensible happiness promised by God.

All humanity—every man, woman, and child, young and old, sick and healthy, the rich, the destitute, the cleric, the layman, the single, and married, every teenager, *every* human being—desires this perfect happiness. This universal desire proves God's existence. For every instinctive craving and longing dwelling within humans on earth there is a corresponding satisfaction. No exception exists. It is therefore impossible to believe that man alone is doomed to frustration; that man must envy all other creatures since they have no appetites that must remain unsatisfied. Our very reason, which marks us distinctively as humans, demands the existence of an infinitely good God whose limitless perfections will completely satisfy every desire of every human heart.

As man conquers outer space, he seems to lose the conquest of self. But the paradox discloses that in exactly the direct proportion in which he masters what exists outside of him, he himself seems to become enslaved *on the inside*. He experiences an *imprisonment of the soul*. As we look about the planet Earth, as others as well have done in the past with greater or lesser degrees of investigation, we note that modern humanity is living in jeopardy of losing its personal salvation. Probably a more accurate self-analytical question could be posed: DOES THE DISTRACTING WORLD IN WHICH WE LIVE, WITH ALL ITS MATERIALISTIC BEAUTY AND ATTRACTIONS, DEAFEN AND DEADEN MAN'S INSIGHT TO AN INEVITABLE FACT; DOES MAN NOT REALIZE THAT HE HAS A SOUL TO SAVE?

The days that make up weeks, the weeks that accumulate into years pass very quickly, quickly indeed! Infancy toddles into childhood; childhood pranks converge into teenage spirits of adventure; adolescence surrenders to the care of both pain and pleasure, sorrow and joy; adulthood ages into the various phases of new wisdom to what was and what is.

Who am I? Why have I been here? Is there any life beyond ALL THIS? Yes, life passes by very swiftly. All too soon are memories passed along into the eternal archives. To the young, the future seems so far away. "I wish I were twenty," says the ten-year-old. At twenty, twenty-one, or twenty-two, the hard knocks of living in a world at struggle offer a traumatic blow: reality can be harsh. Oh, to be youthful again, when the cares and the woes of life are handled by those disciplined through the winters and summers of their own days!

The present as soon as it is a *present* becomes a past. Each new present, born from its past, focuses to the future: days of uncertainty, perhaps pressure and stress. One even looks at the future while recalling scars already acquired. Where has life gone? Why was life experienced as such? Where can I rest my weary heart, my fretting mind, my jaded emotions, my fatigued body? If it be true that I a human have been endowed with an immortal soul, incorruptible with an everlasting existence, what then will happen if I lose my soul *forever and forever* in an agelessness of eternity? ETERNITY! . . . where man has a beginning and no end.

3.

We Come as Beggars Do—in Hope

Hope, like the gleaming taper's light,
Adorns and cheers our way;
And still, as darker grows the night,
Emits a brighter ray.
OLIVER GOLDSMITH, "The Traveller"

Is there a survival virtue? The crises of our modern world have brought many responsible minds to a concerned search for genuine ethical and moral values. Men of thought and power have attempted to make this quest into the depths of human hearts; for perhaps in the human who is constantly in a voyage of discovery for happiness there could exist the very roots of an answer to such crises.

These values have not been totally recognized by our materialistic population because the "modern mind" is absorbed neurotically and psychotically in itself. Moreover, it has as a society imprisoned itself within its own egocentric walls. It has forgotten where to find the key to escape and freedom. In its imprisonment, if the modern mind would only look to the open window, it would, like the poet Frederick Langbridge, see the stars. It would rediscover "the sure and firm anchor" of HOPE. St. Paul, in Hebrews 6:19, speaks of two irrevocable assurances, about which there could be no question of God deceiving us. These are His promises of hope and encouragement if we persevere.

In an attempt to give focus to humanity's "blurred vision," Christianity has throughout the ages offered values. Sometimes, however, and sadly so, the Christian orthodoxy has appraised humanity's dim-sighted ethical and moral illness with a cold eye. This appraisal is natural for a civilization that gears itself to and limits its vision to the physical and the technological. How unfortunate that a materialistic age has rejected the spiritual. This crisis has magnified before conscientious minds and national leaders the esteem for the constant values that authentic Church authorities promulgate and protect.

The message of the Gospel is powerful! The message of the Gospel is perennial as it is Divine. The Gospel message is social as it is personal; it is all-encompassing. The Gospel message inspires faith that sustains love; but it is HOPE that sustains the love produced through that FAITH. God intends to bring about "a people." That is all God ever wanted to do: to form "a people." When that happens, there will be no longer a need for teachers, preachers, healers, and evangelists.

But until that day comes, God brings His people into oneness by the message of Hope which is the message of the Gospel. Hope is brought to us by the preaching of the Faith. How can we learn and believe, how can we live aright unless there is someone to preach? Paul in his message to the Hebrews stresses this well. Beautiful and lofty are his thoughts on Faith—Faith right from the beginning of time to this very moment—which will bring God's people into "healing as a people, and healing as a nation." But how is this to be accomplished according to Paul? He asks the rhetorical question: How are people to have faith unless there be someone to preach to them the good news of Faith, Love, and Hope?

As we know, God has not left us as orphans. He has not left us with a goal but no map; He has not given us a destiny but no voice to urge us onward. In every moment of history, God raises voices: men and women on fire with the love of God and the passionate desire to proclaim the Good News. John Paul II vibrantly preached: "Let the evangelist present himself as one whose sole 'journey of faith' produces the proclamation of the Gospel, the strengthening of brothers, the consoling of the afflicted, the bearing of witness to God's love, the pointing out to mankind its transcendental destiny. May it allow those who hear to forever remember this experience in their minds, wills, and hearts."

Desperately we need hope along the way. Every period of history has had its own distinctive need of hope; ours is no different except for the times, the circumstances, and the people. HOPE IS A SURVIVAL VIRTUE! It sees beyond the "blue horizon" to an Almighty Power who can change dismal rain into a rainbow of sunshine and blessings. HOPE IS AN ADVENTURE! Hope breaks through storms; it breaks through clouds! It is an adventure of discovery as it marches victoriously through the hardships and problems of time. Hope sees the stars not the mud. Hope looks up not down! Hope produces VICTORS, namely, those who have attained. Hope discloses courageous persons with VISION! Yes, a vision beyond and above the present sorrow. Moreover, persons of hope are exemplars, to be not only admired but emulated.

An old man once said when one loses love, he sins. When one loses faith, he rankles. When one loses hope, he dies! On the other hand, repentance can make love return. A peak experience can renew faith. But it takes resurrection to restore hope.

Hope is a beautiful power! Hope has the fire to radiate light over darkness. Hope offers much more than the weight of probabilities. It represents reality-conquest. It is self-verifying. It not only places one's feet on solid ground, it illuminates footpaths to be followed along a road. In its strength there is vim, vigor, and vitality, which become what the world of today needs so much: A WAY OF LIFE!

4.
The Healing Hope

Are you in search of hope? Well, I have a message for you. HOPE IS IN SEARCH OF YOU! Psalm 39:7 tells us: "So tell me, Lord, what can I expect? My hope is in you." Again the Scriptures encourage us with exciting hope in the words: "Hear and answer my prayer, O Lord, and let me not weep in vain." St. Paul, too, is so very encouraging. He once said to the Corinthians: "We suffer all kinds of afflictions and yet we are not overcome. For ourselves, we are being hampered everywhere, yet still have room to breathe, are hard put to it, but never at a loss; persecution does not leave us unbefriended, nor crushing blows destroy us; we carry about continually in our bodies the dying state of Jesus, so that the living power of Jesus may be manifested in our bodies too." (Knox) (2 Cor. 4:8–11) Then in Romans 8:20, he adds: "Creation is made subject to futility . . . by Him who once subjected it, yet not without hope." *(NAB)*

Hope is in the future. Faith is in the present. It is my prayer to enkindle a holy fire within you—to lead you to the feet of Jesus, that you may place total and unconditional faith in Him. He is the son of God. He is real! He came and He suffered and died for you, for me. Before He was killed, He did many, many good things: preaching about the Kingdom, forgiving the weaknesses of humanity, healing every sort of human ailment. He was so perfectly good that only goodness could issue from Him. And so, in this chapter on healing hope, I offer you the Hope of all mankind: I offer you Jesus. He is the hope of all living. He alone is the hope of all nations! He alone will wipe away your tears. He alone can make you whole. He alone can give you peace. He alone; He alone; and only He is Hope PERSONIFIED!

Nobody, nothing has the power to destroy you. Only you can destroy yourself. But if you can destroy yourself, you can also surrender your trust in yourself to the power of God; and God can then build you up to a new creation. That's what the power of God can do for you. And so, in the brokenness of your present being, no matter what it may be, no matter what your brokenness may have done to you, you can have Divine

Hope for a better tomorrow. You do this with a "better you" which only God through Jesus can accomplish.

Hope is the least spoken-about power; and yet on the other hand, it is the strength most needed. That is why it is an underpinning to this whole book. Besides consulting many of my philosophy and theology texts, notes, and lectures, as well as reviewing many notations from my own personal prayer moments with God, I went to the good old reliable dictionary to find out about hope. Webster's New International Dictionary, second edition, defines "hope" as:

1. Desire accompanied with expectation of obtaining what is desired, or belief that it is obtainable

2. Ground or source of happy expectation, hence, a good promise

For the present purpose, hope is regarded as a Divine Gift embedded in the nature of every man and woman and child. It enables people to seek realistic desired goals. As with all gifts, it can be taken for granted and never really understood. But hope is that small spark, that smoldering, suppressed flame, kindling our insides, that will not be extinguished. As Simon, the ragpicker, said in Og Mandino's book *The Greatest Miracle in the World:* "There is always hope. When all hope is gone the world will end."

Hope is part of life itself, helping us in time of trial. For man constantly yearns for something more, for something beyond his natural reach. Hope for a better expectation in our personal lives and in that of society must of necessity look to Faith in Christ. Again St. Paul proclaims in Hebrews 7:19: "Instead, a fuller hope has been brought into our lives, enabling us to come close to God." This is strong language! This is strong hope! It is a hope that flows only from faith in God's loving Providence. Faith nourishes our hope with the constancy of God's promises recorded in the testimony of Sacred Scripture.

Hope in God has two facets. Both flow from the Divine Love for you and for me. (1) God has concern for you! and (2) Because you are in need, because you feel insecure, you must trust. Along life's way, people at some time or other need to trust. Truth will bring us to the shores of Hope. There, after having drifted on the stormy seas of life's journeys, we are salvaged. We are thankful we have survived. We still have a chance "to live anew." Hope comes alive. It produces in people courage to go on. It brings spiritual peace as it instructs and convinces, as it encourages and comforts. In this game of living it seems that a person can never have too much confidence in his or her God. St. Teresa of the Child Jesus, that trusting little Carmelite nun, used to say: "As we hope, so shall we receive."

St. Augustine, so well known for his honest confessions, used to say: "Our hearts shall not rest until they rest in thee." To paraphrase Webster's definition, therefore, hope is to possess what is desired or promised, or what faith says is obtainable. The strongest words flow right from the mouth of St. Paul: "It is that which gives substance to our hopes, which convinces us of the things we cannot see; to have faith is to be sure of the things we hope for, and to be certain of the things we cannot see." That SOMETHING MORE is Christ and immortality. The cycle is complete: LIFE—DEATH—CHRIST—RESURRECTION—NEW BIRTH!

The only thing man is humanly certain of in this world is death. Yet Jesus Christ proclaims with Divine Authority: "I tell you most solemnly, everybody who believes has eternal life." (John 6:47) What powerful words! Can you imagine? Eternal life! How can this be? Everything around us eventually dies. Throughout the Scriptures, however, the Divine Words and Deeds bespeak an existence that is immortal and everlasting. Comparing a person's mortal and brief life against a never-ending existence certifies how insignificant time on earth is unless a person receives it as God's gift and uses it for growth in the Divine Love Plan. What an expectation! What a promise!

What would become of a human being if that person refused God? Without God, and all that the Divine represents, you and I would be reduced to only a refined sophisticated animal with a finite life. Think about that. A man without hope! A woman without a destiny! A child without a future! Everything would be terminal to the ground. All human beings would be just passing years without any hope; they would find themselves totally frustrated because they would be filled with real and tremendous desires and no expectation of fulfillment.

All this should remind us how much we need God. God is the Hope of our happiness. He is our Creator and we need Him for our salvation. This is His world. He made it and He has a right to direct it as He planned. We are part of that plan. He wants us to cooperate naturally in fulfilling that plan. And in so doing we will find our own infinite perfection. He will give us the power and we will give Him the glory.

God gave us Jesus to show us how to give that glory to our Father, our Creator. Our Lord Jesus became our redeemer. In so becoming human, Jesus became the Hope of our salvation. What Our Lord persistently asks from His disciples, and the first thing He requested from His chosen twelve, is faith. "Believe in me." But the belief He sought was not mere intellectual acceptance of His words; it had to be a trustful, a hopeful living behavior that acknowledged God's supreme power and dominion over them. It had to be a total surrender, a total submission of our reason, the best and noblest of our faculties. With unquestionable hope you and I are asked to accept Him and His teachings.

When we make this act of trust, we proclaim hope in God as creator. We are witnessing that God has created all things for good; all things for their greatest good; and everything for its own good. What might be good for you might not be good for another. And the Creator has determined that unless you interfere with His plan you should reach your greatest happiness. You are very special to Him. He calls you by name. We leave everything to Him; we must leave all to Him.

And so, we cling to the promise that Hope *is* our God/our Creator. We desperately hold on to Hope especially when we are tempted to see ourselves as merely dragging through dense woodlands, trodding, groping, wandering as in a darkened forest, questioning whether the Father has set us adrift. But then comes this strong desire seeking a future good, this driving force that leads us to place our fulfillment in Christ. We know confidently that we will not be abandoned to worldly conflicts, injustices, insecurities, and war. Our words, our attitudes, our actions should witness to Christian hope, not to despair.

The Fisherman Apostle exhorts all Christians (1 Pet. 3:14–16) until the end of time to readily give reason for their hope: "If you do have to suffer for being good, you will count it a blessing. There is no need to be afraid or to worry about them. Simply reverence the Lord Christ in your hearts, and always have your answer ready for people who ask you the reason for the hope that you all have. But give it with courtesy and respect and with a clear conscience, so that those who slander you when you are living a good life in Christ may be proved wrong in the accusations that they bring."

5.
I Have a Value for You

There is a "best" in you that is yet to be. Don't you know that? The reason you are sometimes, as the modern saying goes, "down in the dumps" is precisely because way down deep in your inner being, your inner sanctum, there is imprisoned the beautiful you who wants to believe that YOU ARE FREE just because God has made you free! You were meant to be released from the burdens of life, from those dragging, sullen, morose influences that make you despair rather than rejoice in the privilege to be alive! God created the best in you. God wants that best to bloom for YOU and for HIS GLORY. God gave you power for your hour. God gave you your hour for His glory. When you use it you will find personal achievement; better still, you will BE.

Let God release you from yourself. What is your prison? What is your hang-up? What have you done to yourself? What has society, what has your church done to you? These call for very personal answers. Many times we become, as some philosophers state, what we receive from another only to the extent that we interpret it and make it our own. The principle is: whatever is received is received by another according to the makeup of the receiver. Ask God right now . . . right now as you read these pages . . . to make you be RELEASED TO BE FREE!

In reading this book you will likewise have the opportunity to fully realize your relation with God—a God who is good, a God who loves you, a God who is always in search of you, a loving Father with many gifts for you! With humility, leading to the desire to becoming better, (realizing that true wisdom is knowing that we are still in quest), you will be able to understand that there is no moment in your precious life that lacks significance. There exists in you no part of life in which there is no need of union with the Source of life. Recognizing through the years of experience that such a union is God's constant will for us, we—all of us —cannot admit that this union is impossible, or even difficult.

This book leads you hopefully to God as it leads you honestly into yourself—to union of mind and heart, to a better knowledge of God and a greater insight into yourself. These values make us free. These values help us to fulfill the requisites for sanctity. And sanctity is our basic inner craving: We want *to be*—not just to achieve—the very best in ourselves.

VALUES! Just what are they? Values come in all sizes and shapes. But essentially they are immutable. Some might understand them as valor, courage. Others may observe them as measurement, estimates. Men and women of art and thought might look upon value as a degree, as a hue, as an appraisal. In relation to the passions one can sense them as dearness, honor, love, respect. Those who might slip up in life's ways feel in their consciences the absence of value; they might feel it as cheapness, as something trivial or profitless. Yes, there are many sorts of values. But the one thing they share in common is their essential *worth*. You are worth something! And you respond to that worth by living your values.

In appreciating the influence of values, it is necessary for the soul to read slowly and reflectively. When delving into unchangeable values, one also should observe that regardless of revolutionizing, transforming times, values remain both steadfast and stable.

Values never represent novelties. Values do not betray a human person with whimsical experiences that flicker out quickly. You can derive value from this reading by not rushing through it as you would a detective novel. The best profit comes from peacefully stopping and dwelling at the well of insight. Drink from the well! Satiate your thirst with God's creation of important you! Learn and appreciate, accept and vitalize the promises of the Lord.

As you enter within yourself, from the depths of your humanity look up to the Divine for resurrection and a life that is worth living. It is my healing prayer that these reflections convince you that being created by a loving Heavenly Father means IT IS GREAT TO BE YOU! Furthermore, be assured—once and for all—that YOU ARE NOT A functionary! People are not functionaries! Let the message of these chapters, written after much prayer and retreat reflections, many times before the Blessed Lord's holy presence in the tabernacle, make you AUTHENTIC. If you do, you will have made a voyage of valuable, profound discovery: the beauty of God's care for you. WITH FAITH YOU WILL CREATE SOMETHING VISIBLE FROM THE HIDDEN INVISIBLE YOU!

PART II
The Value of
the Individual

6.

The Soul

Life is the soul's nursery—
Its training place for the
Destinies of eternity.

THACKERAY

As a priest, I am interested in one thing alone; nothing else matters. *I AM INTERESTED IN YOUR SOUL!* I cannot help but recall a passage collected and placed at random among my daily scribblings. It deals with "immortality," and expresses these thoughts: RELEASE—Man is like a bird in a cage until he lives for eternity. He is like a prisoner in a cell until he gives expression to the eternal within him. Just as the ripples of the meadow brook reproduce the swell of the ocean tides toward which the brook flows; and just as the music of the rivulet in its eddies echoes the lap of the mighty sea on the beach where some day the rivulet will measure its waters; so the voices within us are the voices of the larger life for which we are destined and toward which we are going.

Does this not speak of the immortality of the soul? Whether one realizes it or not, one's human soul cries for its God. It needs its God like a rose seeking its most beautiful day of days in full bloom as it craves nourishment from the earth and sunshine from the heavens. It is like a fish that cannot survive out of water. A soul in union with God will always be in springtime; but it can in no way survive without its God. St. Augustine was so exact when he uttered that he could not live unless he lived with his Maker. Without God accepted and living in a human soul, that soul will undergo a great crisis because it will be starving itself from the source of its life.

When a person has spent much of his life pursuing materialistic or secularistic goals, it becomes difficult to explain to him in his adult years precisely what his soul should mean to him. Often preconceptions from earlier years must be removed before one is in a position to appreciate what the soul should be in the life of a maturing human being. But God's love is so compulsory, so intense a love that He will receive His creatures whenever they come, regardless of their condition. Love has no limitations to its embrace. And God is Love. And we are lovable because He has created us with immortal souls for Him and Him alone.

Every age has somehow spoken of this "inner principle" of vitality, this thing not to be weighed or measured, yet not to be doubted in the graphic facts of life. It is interesting to read, moreover, how even Greek mythology adds its spice in proof of the existence of the soul. The story is recorded that Psyche, lovely princess, most beautiful to behold, fell in love with Eros (Cupid), the son of Aphrodite (Venus). It is one of the best-known tales in the mythology of ancient Greece. Her beauty was extraordinary, beyond description—so much so that the goddess Venus became jealous of her. Venus ordered Cupid to make Psyche fall in love with some ugly person. However, when Cupid gazed upon this enchantingly beautiful girl, he became so startled that he accidently pricked himself with one of his own arrows. That wound became the enrapturing wound of profound unquenchable love. And so he married her. Secretly he kept her in his palace. He visited her every night. But Psyche never saw her husband. If she were ever to look upon him and see him, Cupid would be obliged to leave her, so he warned.

One night, Psyche was determined to see her husband. Love craves the vision of the one loved. And with this eager desire, after he had fallen asleep, she shone her lamp upon him. As she feasted her vision upon Cupid, she was overwhelmed by this handsome young god. Surprised and overcome, she accidently spilled a drop of hot oil from her lamp on his shoulder. Cupid awakened and vanished.

In her grief, Psyche went to Venus and begged to see her husband again. So Venus compelled her to undergo three hard tasks. The last of these caused her death. The story continues that Cupid, because of his immense love for Psyche, brought her back to life. Then he begged Zeus (Jupiter) to make Venus forgive both of them. Jupiter did, and he gave Psyche immortality as well.

The story concludes by moralizing that Cupid represented the heart, and Psyche was to be the human soul. Her onus and her struggles, her sorrow and her pain were indicative of all the trials and adversities the human soul must undergo on earth. And so it came to be that the word "psyche" means "soul."

And so, you live! And your consciousness of your own self is the very first proof of the life within your being. This is your soul! Sometime or somewhere during the days of your life, your mind must have entertained the questions: "What am I? Am I alive?" These powers ushering forth from within your humanity, where have they sprung from? As you observe yourself, you are conscious of yourself as being responsible for initiating your personal activities. You are aware also of various behaviors, of those going on in the world about you. You possess understanding, will power, feeling, heart and emotional sensitivities. Your imagination can build castles in the sky. The spirit of adventure and enterprise compel you to investigate pathways perhaps never before trodden. Your social needs elicit the sharing of your desires with other human beings who act out their own dramas on the stage of life. You observe your body with all its levels of growth and its fascinating strength. How sensitive, indeed, it is to touch and smell, to hear and see! To be able to walk wherever I would go satisfies my spirit of liberty as I search for my very own fortune.

It is interesting to observe how this body, this physical structure and substance, strives incessantly to attain and retain its health, strength, and beauty. Yet, in spite of these lofty aspirations, the intruding enemy of sickness and disease startles us into the grim reality and inevitable truth: LIFE IS FRAGILE AS IT IS PRECIOUS!

LIFE! What a remarkable gift! But from whom does this gift come? What is this thing called LIFE? It is indeed a perplexity. Some look upon life as a property that distinguishes living organisms from dead organisms and nonliving matter, shown in the ability to grow, metabolize, respond to stimuli, and reproduce. Others consider life as a period of time between conception or birth and death. To other minds, life is perceived as activity in general. The biblical concept is more comprehensive and most sacred in its holistic concept of life both in general and in particular. According to Sacred Scripture, the universe was created in six days. This account is absolutely correct and cannot be doubted. The word "day," however, does not necessarily indicate twenty-four hours; rather, it helped the people to grasp the idea that there were six phases, or periods, of creation.

We would never be convinced of the story of creation unless God had chosen to reveal it to us. The Creator alone knows fully the truth about creation. Science has offered various interpretations of how and when the earth came into being. One teaching is that it broke forth from a hot mass of volcanic eruptions about four and a half billion years ago. Water overflowed everything. Vapor finally condensed from this, forming oceans, and they in turn evaporated repeatedly and condensed for hundreds of millions of years, due to the intense heat. When the oceans cooled to about a hundred and forty degrees, life was possible. This event, according to some scientists, occurred probably two billion years ago, and the life formed was a simple organism. Mammals and animals seem to have appeared on earth about one hundred and fifty million years ago. Man in all probability made his advent on earth approximately two million years ago. There are certain scientists who deny God and His revelation, and in consistency with their theory proclaim an uncertainty about the origin of both the world and man. But God has not hidden the truth of Creation from mankind. He has revealed it in the very first account of the Bible, the book of Genesis. It is not my intent to get bogged down with statistics and scientific theories. I wish, though, to focus on the Author of all life.

Sacred Scripture is part of history and tells us very clearly that God created the world and all things springing forth in it and from it. The word "create" indicates making something out of nothing. Never in the Scriptures is the power to create attributed to mankind. When man makes a thing he does so with previously existing matter. In Genesis we see that man's universe is not a creation of the heavens and the earth, the water and the land, the sun and the moon, the plants and the animals all at once. God's creative power unfolded these creations at different intervals. None of these created things came into existence by themselves.

Further, Genesis does not tell us at what precise date man made his appearance on the earth. Nor does it disclose the period of time God took in developing man's body to receive directly the human soul created by the Almighty. But it leaves absolutely no doubt as to man's origin: Man was created by God who breathed into him a human soul, the breath of life. God made man lesser than the angels. God "spirited" man with a principle of life that would continue forever even after the body decayed. By means of this immortal soul God made man to His own image and likeness. Man could think and choose freely. By means of this "gift of life," so special indeed, man became the master of the earth. And then all things upon this universe of earth and skies would come under his dominion.

What follows from this is that the true glory of man resides not in the powers of his body. But his soul bears the glory of its creation, and it will some day go back to God. Man's destiny is not dust. His life, full and complete, is for eternity. Without this fulfillment, man is going against his very nature, his very purpose. Those who fight and deny this destiny will find, as the poet, Francis Thompson, put it, that all things betray

them who betray God. Man cannot be happy apart from God. We may
seek life elsewhere, but it will be found in no one but God. He is the
Divine Life—the only life we seek.

Life on earth will always emerge and unfold as one of the great myster-
ies of the universe. The question, "What is life?" will probably be one of
the deepest questions we can ask. It also remains—even as it does unfold
itself moment by moment, age by age—the greatest mystery confronting
us. Life has no simple definition!

We perceive that a bird sings, and thus it is alive! We joyfully behold
the miracle of the rose in its few days of glory; but soon, very soon, it
withers away from its moment of beauty into the sleep of death. We gaze
up to the mountain. There it stands so majestically: tall, overpowering,
wide, and strong! Yet, it has no life within itself. The ages of time,
through wind and force, storm and friction, slowly erode it. We identify
living things by certain behavior patterns; we are awestruck at the sight
of living things in growth, in self-reproduction. We distinguish living
things from nonliving things in the way the substances that compose
them are put together. From that initial moment of the first man and
woman, investigation of this life—its cause, activity, and end—has stimulated the continuous inquiries: Who is man? Why is he here? Where is he
going?

The earth is at our disposal. We can examine the living creatures,
observing their sizes, shapes, and the regions in which they live, to ascer-
tain the common denominator of relationship. These common qualities
make up life; we classify all living things as either plant or animal. But
regardless of how much accumulative knowledge we record, we remain
baffled about the soul and what life itself actually is.

A lay teacher once said to the children in his school that the soul
which was the principle of life was only blood; and to convince them, he
drew a drop of blood from the most courageous boy and then asked him,
"If instead of taking out one drop of blood, I take it all out, will you
live?"

"No, sir."

"Will you die?"

"Yes, sir," replied the boy.

"Do you understand now how blood is the soul that gives life to the
body?"

"No, sir," said the boy who was more cunning than the teacher.

"Why do you say no?"

"Because although pigs are killed by having their blood taken out, men also die with all the blood in their body."

The dumbfounded teacher refused to give the boy the prize he had promised, saying that he had not given the correct answer.

And so, although living things grow, replace and repair parts of themselves, even adapt to environment and respond to stimuli, in the final analysis, this does not tell what life is. All it discloses are the qualities that things must have to be considered alive.

A plant has a soul: life. But a plant is not human life. It exists only and as long as it is able to extract sustenance from other created, material substances. Earthly existence remains the same in principle: all created beings, by their very nature, are corruptible; they decay and perish. So, too, an animal has a soul: an animal life. It not only contains within its essential totality the vegetative living by which it too can nourish itself, grow, and reproduce, but it bears essentially as part of itself a distinctive nature of sentient life. It can taste, smell, feel, touch, experience pain and pleasure; it can be conditioned and trained to respond automatically to stimuli. But it can never understand the *meaning* of things. It cannot grasp the concepts of beauty, justice, mercy, and love. It is not a human being. When the animal dies, its life too passes into nonbeing.

Man, however, is different—the most remarkable of all creatures. His abilities far surpass those of the plant and the animal. He is the only intelligent creature that can live in all climates. He fabricates and utilizes tools, makes fire from flint and stone. He channels fire into controlled heat and energy. He thinks, reasons, speaks, laughs, prays to a Supreme Being. He recognizes through his own fear of the universe that he is a creature, and therefore, dependent. These unique characteristics make him essentially separate. The most distinctive characteristic, however, is his spirituality. Because he is an intellectual creature, he understands beauty, goodness, justice—all the transcendental qualities and virtues. And it is this spiritual side of man's nature that is called *soul.* The soul that has been given existence by God is not only born into this world, but it lives on forever. There is no limitation to man's knowledge. His earthly life will cease; but there is no ceasing of life in eternity.

Shakespeare's Hamlet says it beautifully: "What a piece of work is a man! how noble in reason! how infinite in faculty! in form and in moving how express and admirable! in action how like an angel! in apprehension how like a god! the beauty of the world! the paragon of animals!" (II, 2, 303–7)

But the finest description of man is found in the words of Psalm 8:5–8:

> *You have made him little less than a god,*
> *you have crowned him with glory and splendor,*
> *made him lord over the work of your hands,*
> *set all things under his feet,*
> *sheep and oxen, all these,*
> *yes, wild animals too,*
> *birds in the air, fish in the sea*
> *traveling the paths of the ocean.*

God placed tremendous beauty within the human soul. This beauty has given birth to such literary artists as Shakespeare and Dickens, musical geniuses as Wagner and Beethoven, artists of paint and canvas as Raphael and Michelangelo. It seems that the soul of man is in continuous search of unity with some being beyond all beings. In the final analysis, man realizes that he must have been made for the heavens; the soul harbored within our body yearns for the BEST.

Our life indeed belongs to God. With our freedom, an abiding expression of our higher spiritual nature, we operate within the framework of our destiny. We are free to deliberate, make decisions, and choose between alternatives. Unlike the animals, we possess freedom to do good or do evil, to abuse God directly, to debase our own personhood, to violate the rights of other persons. But in the end, after the opportunity to live our lives well, the Divine Summons will call each of us into eternity. In that moment, the stroke of death cuts off any further alternative. Each of us, rich or poor, noble or common, clergy or lay, then looks into an eternity of bliss with Him who is the purpose of our existence, or into eternal unhappiness in separation from Him.

When reality of life and death is reviewed, man looks back upon his days. In an attempt to unify himself he discerns his being as having lived on earth with a soul and a body. Recalling his life experiences of "self," he is struck again by the reality that the soul and the body are not loosely connected parts of himself; they are united in a substantial union to form one complete human being. The soul is not located in any particular member of the body, but is whole and entire in each part.

It is both joyful and exciting to delve into our inner selves, to be able to try and understand the marvel of human creation in all its splendor. If we would but only enter within ourselves in all honesty and humility, we would see clearly that GOD IS LOVE AND HE SHARES HIS LOVE IN US THROUGH LIFE: AND WE, TOO, CARRY ON THAT LIFE AS WE SHARE HIS LIFE IN US WITH OTHERS!

A French philosopher once stated that no man is strong unless he bears within his character antitheses clearly marked. We can either love or we can hate. Hate is the opposite of love. But life is best as a creative synthesis of opposites. It can produce fruitful harmony. Those things that offend mortally are perceived to be destructive forces and must be hated. Other things are to be loved as they reflect the Author of all being. All things created are to receive our loving admiration, never our hurtfulness or abuse. We see instead the beauty they reflect from Him above. Our God is more a Father/Abba who is desirous of a good world. But because of man's free will He sometimes appears almost helpless to His own creation in the face of evil forces. Yet, this God of Love creates a world of being outside of Himself, while sharing Himself through the Divine Force of permitted existence.

The soul of man is like God because it is a spirit having understanding and free will. It is destined; it has a purpose. Humans are especially like God when they know and love Him. First, in a merely natural way without the aid of grace. Second, they can know Him in a supernatural way here on earth, with the aid of grace. Third, they come to know Him in a perfect way in heaven, with the aid of the special light God gives to the souls of the blessed.

WHAT A GIFT! A gift, as we have already seen, is something given, endowed; a special talent, aptitude, faculty, quality, attribute. It is a special expression of the person sharing. Our Creator, Our God, Our Father gifts humanity with understanding. He endows each man and woman with this spiritual power to apprehend, to judge, to reason, and thus to know right and wrong. The faculty of conscience becomes each person's capacity to judge. We can decide here and now what should be done as good or avoided as evil.

The most magnificent of all human gifts is FREE WILL. What a sovereign faculty! It can affirm or negate. It is the effectiveness of the soul to choose either to act or not to act. This execution/acting mirrors and rebounds into eternity: human souls live precisely because they are spirits. Their earthly existence is merely a prelude to the agelessness of eternity. As a spirit it is a being, a reality of existence, with understanding and freedom, but no body; *it will never die!* The soul of man is this spirit.

Man's material body may cease to function biologically and chemically; but because man is precisely spirit, he will not die!

These then are some of the wonders of our humanity. So very often we take them for granted; we even become blind to them. Nevertheless, the fact remains that we live by a life that is totally and essentially and dramatically different from any other life in the physical universe. God's masterpiece of Creation in this physical universe is ourselves. To appreciate this masterwork of Divine Genius, it is necessary to identify ourselves in it without ever confusing ourselves with any part of it.

There are people who cannot fathom "immortality"—the never-ending life of the soul. In fact—for any number of reasons—they deny that they have a soul. But no sane person will deny he or she is alive. The soul is the life-giving principle in any living thing. In humans, specifically, the soul is the intellectual principle by which a person knows and chooses. Both philosophy and theology substantiate the human understanding of the soul. Philosophy renders an explanation through natural reason as its fundamental criterion in expounding truth. Theology, a higher science, appeals to God's Word to enlighten man's natural reasoning through Divine Revelation.

Why have I spoken at such length about the soul? The answer simply is because the soul is sacred, it is fragile, and it has value! If the soul were not these, then much time, money, and effort have been needlessly expended through humanitarian causes, through Christian efforts to assist and to embellish the humanities. In empty crucibles have we placed time and money to rehabilitate the criminal, to attempt through medical means to prolong human life amid sickness and excruciating diseases. Social services, medicine, halls of learning, nursing homes, sanitariums would be looked upon only as epicureans at a feast, parasites. A Mother Teresa would be an insane person wasting her life and the lives of her followers—fools to the highest degree!

The question is momentous as it is acute. The answer is penetrating as it is poignant. It is found in the respect and love God has for you, for me. God has made you and me to know Him, to love Him, to serve Him in this world, and to be happy with Him forever in the next! The immortal soul is of highest value. Christian immortality involves the *whole person.*

Inspired religion has always instructed that existence is God-oriented. Our Creator dictates our reason for being. True religion, moreover, must be holistic—it must recognize that human beings are composed of a body and a soul; and that the soul is more important than the body, although the body must be cared for reasonably and conscientiously.

In our search for happiness, then, the soul's end must be of primary importance to us. The desires of the body, its emotions, and so forth, sometimes get in the way of the soul, however. They become genuine obstacles in fulfilling our happiness here and hereafter. But we recognize our imperfections and acknowledge that God alone is perfect. Full happiness is attainable only by living our lives in accord with God's regulations and dictates. These are made known to us through conscience and through religion. For this reason, one can see that all human people are bound to find the Christian family that most closely resembles the mind of God. When they find it, they are bound to live it to its full. God, through His Divine Providence, has revealed this through His Divine Son, Jesus Christ. Our Blessed Lord taught not only verbally along the shores and Palestinian hills, but also through His signs and wonders, that our major occupation, to which every other preoccupation should be subject, is the saving of our souls! Striving for perfection by avoiding wrong makes us eligible for sainthood.

Unfortunately, there are occasions when the body seeks its own interests; it divests itself from the soul's interest. The body, then, driven by its own cravings, seeks its own comfort. This is understandable; because the body, unlike the soul, does not have intellectual insight, nor volition. It has passions—anger, pride, avarice, covetousness, envy, lust—that burst forth like the flames from a burning volcano.

One must not, however, conclude that the body is evil. No! God created the body. And it too is good. The body and the soul are not dual forces in opposition to each other. On the contrary. In the Scriptures, God has revealed to us that the soul is a power of the body. Psychology itself, moreover, emphasizes the importance of this mutual relationship. St. Thomas Aquinas championed both these theses as "principle of life." What is basically being said is that both body and soul make distinctive contributions to the totality of mankind. Because of original sin and its consequences, attempting to live in a God-like way, attempting to adhere staunchly to the teachings and the spirit of Christ, appears to be a herculean challenge; but it is really possible.

Our healing evangelism programs of prayer and teaching bring the compassion and love of God, of Christ, God's Son, to those who are struggling. Offering companionship is really sharing the pain by *being* those who suffer. When people observe us caring for them, they become convinced of two basic facts: that human beings with similar problems have a deeper love within them which makes God evermore present as He really is—a God of love; second, that God has sent these humans to the forlorn as His channels of visible love mustering them to realize the value of their immortal souls. Seeing that God cares, observing another human person extending that love, stirs people to become good Christians. Experiencing the compassionate love of Christ, who suffered and died and rose again for the sake of humanity's soul, transforms past sloth into spiritual energy and soul-saving virtue.

In following God we may at times be mocked and laughed at. We may experience persecution in thought, word, and deed from those who would remain agnostic and godless. But each one of us comes to the reality of his or her soul when we constantly and preventively care for the body. Somehow each one knows that the life principle of activity dwells within. It is so comforting to read the Scriptures, to hear holy persons speak of how God through His Son sends healing, and how we in turn are to seek health of soul.

Amid today's pressures and stresses in both the economic and social fields, the important fact of "losing one's soul" is either subconsciously disregarded or outrightly and consciously disdained. Our Blessed Lord Himself admonished that the road to damnation is wide as it is easy to follow; and the road to heaven is narrow, as there are few courageous souls to follow, a few to find it. Why? The answer remains always the same: to be holy is a holistic journey into our humanity; going into its very depths, and from those depths to look up with hope to Someone encouraging us upward to Himself. It means a hard journey in life's days —a hodgepodge of ups and downs, and *brokenness*—but a journey supported by the constant Divine Hand of Love Supreme, Healing applied, eternity attained!

To be saved is to invite our God into our being, allowing Him to control our lives—to lead us. And since He has offered, we need only respond. We do this by removing from our mind the very first attack by agnosticism and atheism; and that is the attack against TRUTH. The truth that our souls are a gift from God, living in this material universe, needing spiritual nurturing, and destined for eternity becomes the basis for our lifetime endeavor: to live in a God-like way, to live authentically our Faith, and to witness second by second the values of ethics and revealed morality.

For the Christian, the added confirmation is that Jesus Christ is the

One sent by the Father, the Father who made us, the Father who provides for us, the Father who calls us to claim our inheritance! This imposes an obligation that we need to stand out as different, that we seek God's way and witness to it, that we need to be fearless in contradicting the terrible philosophies and false deities of worldly fabrication, that we need to be intrepid to chagrin and libel. This is what the Blessed Lord meant when He declared: "You have to seek health of soul."

I heartily believe—and preach—that "reality is not touched until someone touches the human soul." Our Blessed Lord Himself weighed this value well when He placed the human soul in its realistic balance: "What will a man gain by winning the whole world, and at the end lose his immortal soul!" How true it is that life is so simple when we do not complicate it. But complicate it we do! Just take a look at our contemporary world, with its concern about material things. Thoughts and endeavors are focused on tremendous projects such as orbiting in space, delving into ways of possible human habitation beneath the sea. But man himself —his inevitable, ultimate conquest—is ignored. By its utter absorption in materialistic interests, *modern humanity is losing its soul!*

Still more lamentable is that a part of modern humanity does not even realize that each man and woman has a soul to be saved. It seems that mankind becomes aware of this truth only when life casts him or her upon a bed of pain, and no human power can offer a healing. But God's love is eternal as God Himself is; His love remains uninterrupted, persistent, and determined.

God will have naught else but the soul He created: *unless* the soul itself repudiates the God of All Living. When man's earthly conquests come to a halt, all that is left to ask is the most important question of all: IS YOUR SOUL SAVED, OR IS YOUR SOUL LOST—FOREVER?

In 1951, while I was a student of philosophy at the major House of Letters of St. Charles Seminary in Staten Island, New York, our classes were permitted to attend a monthly literary forum. Distinguished speakers were selected and invited to share their particular interests. The story that moved me most came directly from the lips of a fallen-away Catholic who had affiliated himself with the atheistic Communist life. He was Louis Budenz, former editor of the Communist *Daily Worker* in New York City. His dramatic story was later narrated in print in *Treasure in Clay,* the autobiography of the renowned Fulton J. Sheen. Budenz related how he was being forcefully rebutted both in print and in speech by the then Monsignor Fulton J. Sheen. Budenz stated that his own party leaders had ordered him to meet privately with "this Sheen" who seemed to know Communist philosophy with exceptional insight. The purpose was perhaps to convert Sheen to the Communist cause. During the conversation (which Archbishop Sheen himself describes in his book), Monsignor Sheen "suddenly" broke the "heavy" conversation. Looking directly into the eyes of Budenz with that special piercing look so characteristic of the clergyman, Monsignor Sheen sharply accosted his challenger: "I don't care about your communism! I CARE ABOUT YOUR SOUL!"

When Budenz returned home, he was very angry. His wife wondered what the clergyman had done or said to perturb him so. Budenz, still infuriated, shouted out: "I hate *that man! I hate that man!* Do you know the audacity he had? Do you know what he said to me? He said he wasn't interested in my communism. He said *he was interested in MY SOUL!* Can you imagine, MY SOUL!"

And that, my readers, is where I leave you at this moment. I am not interested in what you have or are trying to make of yourself in this world; I do not care what you and time have done to yourself. *I AM INTERESTED ONLY IN YOUR SOUL!*

7.
The Most Important Man in the World

Are you the most important man in all the world? Every man wants to be important. Deep within his own being there resides the dreams, the wishes, the ambitions of not only being important, but also of being forever remembered. In each man there are the moments of the agony of defeat; but the great man is one who takes defeat and transforms it into the thrill of victory. This is the man people remember. This type of man inspires. This sort of man has written his name in the pages of stirring accounts to be remembered and retold. The man of importance is the gentleman who has faced his moment of truth.

Life is like that. It makes winners and losers. Some people, especially the losers, rather think that their misfortune is just "bad luck." The winners explain their "good luck" as the outcome of hard work. But the man of truth is he who comes to realize that he basically is nothing but a vessel who has been especially blessed by some power from "way up there." Because he believes that "somebody up there loves him," he comes to grips with himself. That "somebody up there" is God. The truth of the matter is that God gives him the strength and courage he needs to meet the challenges of life, be they on or off the battlefield. Such a man is an honest man and it is honesty that makes a man important!

Carl Sandburg, commenting on the centennial anniversary of the Lincoln era, pointed out why some men wax remarkably strong. He indicated that a man, just like Lincoln, can become respected as one of the giants of one's age. In the observations of Sandburg, however, it takes truth and honesty to produce on earth a man who is both steel and velvet, who can be at the same time hard as rock and soft as drifting fog, a man who holds in his heart and mind the paradox of terrible storm and unspeakable peace.

The most interesting man who ever lived is the man who stands tall in truth and in honesty. He has what everyone respects: he is gentle, but this gentleness is combined with terrific toughness. He does not ridicule. He does not run the frantic race for self-emergence through acquiring power. Men will become giants of tremendous strides if they will pause from their hustle and bustle. Silence speaks. Its message is direct, clear, and very honestly simple. The devil's first and primary attack upon mankind is the disruption and the destruction of truth. When truth falls, honesty is no more.

God wants every man to be the most important man in all the world. God never abandons man. The Almighty Voice is *never* still. Forests, lands, seas are his written words; the sound of the breeze, the chattering of the birds echo his creative presence. God speaks pleasantly if man would only take time to listen.

A man needs another human being to communicate with him. Together they share their thoughts, their feelings. And there need be no threat of insecurity or of rejection. Should not both voices be heard? Should not a man listen to a woman's thoughts? If men would listen, they would learn. Unbiased listening has the power to transform. It can muster new horizons, activate latent motivations, even produce *giants!*

Through a thousand different ways women today are desperately trying to speak to men. Women are speaking not out of envy, jealousy, or even resentment. They are not even trying to conquer a man's world. They attempt only to fulfill their natural specialty, namely, *to love.* A distinctive feature of their love is that through their loving a human being, a human person grows. That person matures into Christian liberation. This allows a person to free himself or herself from himself or herself without incurring self-hurt. Then, he or she is socially fit to go forth to assist other human beings to free themselves in the same way.

Men often complain that they are "misunderstood." Occasionally they might be. This is part of human frailty as well as of its folly. A woman discerns that her man, in his own struggle for power and affirmation, is like a frenzied chicken running about, groping, searching. Her man is tired, but through false pride will not admit it. He has been betrayed by life and its promises, but will not accept the fact. She is saddened to see his bruises, his utter folly in contriving and utilizing a host of ridiculous human strengths. He is suffering. But if he would just rest awhile in the requiem of silent prayer with her, and see what he is doing to depersonalize not only himself but her and others around him, he would inevitably come to his senses. In that moment, she can nurse his human wounds through her human understanding and love. In that beautiful moment, God could enter. God would bring restoration and healing.

It is very interesting to see how God allows a woman to restore a man. In this process, both are revitalized, strengthened, and renewed. From breakdown, there springs forth survival.

Man needs a woman's presence. We see God's Divine Providence through a human agency (woman), stripping man of his false gods. Being thus stripped, a man comes to the stark truth of humility. He sees who he really is, and what he has done to himself. He is not too proud of that. And in that virtue of humility, he is born again into the power of humility. He knows without any shadow of a doubt that he is nothing; but in that nothing, if he surrenders to his vocation as God intended him to, he would come to know that each one of us from our nothingness becomes somebody only when we allow God to fill us with His gifts. The truth of the matter is that we have gifts only because we are nothing. And the more we are nothing, the more God can gift us.

A man is worth something when he knows that he was created To Be. It is remarkable how God puts up with us all. God is very patient. In fact, He is patient, patient, and more patient. And in *that* order! It is also wonderful how God provides new life through waste, how He promotes growth through the urgency to survive. And so a woman, in her own need to be affirmed primarily as a woman, then as helpmate, companion, associate, spouse, finds a way to protect herself by helping man to release himself from the variety of his childlike defenses. Every grown-up man still retains in himself the image of the *tin soldier* he so often victoriously played at being. His play battles were real. The enemies were actually advancing. Scratches obtained at play were wounds of blood. Conquest had to be made. Victory had to be sure! Tears could not be shed! The most important man of that moment had to be that soldier of scars. The most important man in the world had to be that wounded man who would return to a fair maiden. She hastened in step to his homecoming. Into his enfolding arms she would plunge. For her he was the greatest man that ever lived.

The greatest man in all the world is the man who has found the *remarkable woman.* Such a woman comes from God. That woman is a gift to that man from the Almighty. Remarkably as God has made her, she does not take her relationship to her man lightly. In her modern attempt to strip man of his "boyish defenses," she is really stripping him not sadistically, but constructively. She helps him *affirm himself* in the basic truth that he is a human person, a male, free and yet *enslaved by the need to love, to laugh, to talk.* In surrendering he in turn will be understood, appreciated, and loved just for who he is!

A man will definitely become the greatest when stripped of his pride he *humbly falls* on his knees in prayer. There and only there does he recognize that the Almighty is his creator, that his creator is his God. All he needs to do to survive, to revive, to relive—*to be born again*—is to accept himself just as he is, and to proclaim personally the Heavenly Father.

One of the characteristics of a great man is that he knows how to receive the anointing of a woman. A woman came to Jesus one day. Jesus was dining with some arrogant personalities. This woman presented herself at the doorway of the house. As she stood there with the sun probably shining from behind and casting her shadow upon the floor, she fell to her knees. Slowly she dragged herself, crawled to the only figure she was interested in. That was Jesus. He had given her compassion at a previous time. She now needed His reassurance. And so without feeling embarrassed by the others present, and having no interest in their gossip, she stopped at the bare feet of Jesus. From the depths of her soul welled sorrow and she shed tears. She washed the Lord's feet with those warm tears. Having no other towel, she wiped His feet with the towel of her crimson red, disheveled hair. From an alabaster vial, she poured precious ointment on His feet. She stood and caressed His head gently with her tender warm hands. She took more oil from her vessel and put it on His hair. She was not afraid to touch this man. This man was her God, her creator, her forgiver. He loved her so; and she could return that love only with unconditional surrender.

As astonishing as the anointing may be, more so is the remarkable symbolism of *pouring into the masculine* the pure love of *the feminine.* Though a man may be suffering in his quest for fame and affirmation, so too there is the feminine crying for release from the sensual dominance of the masculine. Give a woman a chance and she will offer a man the remedy of God's presence. She will anoint his head, which is really his will; she will anoint his feet, which really are his understanding. And in the name of the Lord, in the name of His love, a man will be purified and satisfied. In quietness, the presence of the Almighty Creator will affirm man in confidence.

The greatest man in the world is he who experiences *regeneration.* Regeneration is not possible without love. Regeneration makes such a man into a man of faith. A man of faith is one who has *faith in God.*

Great men have done wonders for both themselves and for others. But the greatest and most unforgettable men are those men who accomplished tremendous feats through a living faith. A man's attitude determines the measure of his worth. The great man lives on the *law of success:* you first must give before you can receive. What lies behind us and what lies before us are tiny matters compared to what lies within us. Within each man the Almighty God has in His wisdom and fairness implanted principles and character traits that each can attain if he would pursue them. The *right of choice* is the greatest power that God can give to His creation. If it is used wisely, any man can become the greatest man that ever lived.

The man of faith is one in whom faith *quickens* spiritual understanding. It is notable that the word "quicken" implies not only resurrection of the dead body, but a *renewal* of strength and vitality of the living body. Peter offers us an example of this *quickening faith.* Peter believed Jesus was the Chosen One to come. But it was his faith that produced his spiritual discernment. When Peter allowed Jesus to become the captain of his fishing boat, he knew that this was not Jesus' profession. But in faith he let Jesus command; and when he did, they launched out into deeper water. Therein they made the catch! It was Peter's faith, and his faith alone, that made him look at the human figure of Jesus and proclaim wholeheartedly, enthusiastically: *"TU ES CHRISTUS!* YOU ARE THE CHRIST!"

Without *quickened faith* people live wholly in the intellect. Generally, people who tend to live wholly and solely in the intellect deny that many can know anything about God. Since they lack discerning faith (quickened faith) *they are blinded and cannot see the invisible. And for this reason they are hindered in bringing forth the Divine Presence.* They just don't have it! They don't have any real power! They lack that Divine Grace that makes one *conscious* of God. You see, faith is God, faith is spirit, faith is the *invisible!*

When a man has such an affirmation of faith, he ends up in the purpose of his greatness: to honor God. Such affirmation of faith, such praise and honor to the invisible Godhead, the Unknown God, will make the Deity alive, *visible,* to the mind. It offers regeneration!

What is needed in mankind today, as it has been in every age since that day when Christ walked among us, is a *fresh baptism of the Holy Spirit.* When human beings, men or women, lose their power they should be baptized by the word of the spirit. If a man surrenders to the spirit of God, he will be one of those giants of humanity. His distinctive memorial

will bear this inscription: MAN OF ACCOMPLISHMENT, ACCU-
RACY, ADAPTABILITY; MAN OF BEAUTY, BRAVERY. He
walked this land in the spirit of cheerfulness, caution, choice, and cleanliness. He was confident and considerate; he was filled with courage, courtesy, and curiosity. He trod forward through the difficult with decision,
determination, devotion, and discipline. Duty held first place for him.
With his fellowmen he demonstrated fairness, forgiveness, faithfulness,
and faith. Generosity, goodwill, and gratitude were his companions. He
worked hard with hope in his heart, humility in his belief. His relatives
and friends as well as those who disagreed with him were always treated
with kindness, justice, leadership, loyalty, and love. His home bore the
marks of moderation, neatness, obligation, orderliness. Patience was not
a stranger to him. He lived for God not only through peacefulness, but
with perception and perseverance, with poise and pioneering; he showed
the power to be patriotic. Purity of soul illumined his reason: these made
him reliant upon God as his fountain of resourcefulness. His life of romance was tempered with respect because he knew that every relation
entailed responsibility. Because he was usually self-controlled, he appreciated relaxation and a healthy sense of humor. He found strength in
service to others, appreciating the virtues of sincerity and steadfastness.
Suffering forged him to be thrifty, tactful, and thoughtful. His values
were not destroyed through any selfishness. His most cherished wealth
had its foundation in the wisdom of God through the ages. With God-
power and his own goodwill, there was no evidence of his loss of youth-
fulness.

The most important man in all the world necessarily has to be the man
who is a composite of all the qualities God wants to develop in the lives
of all believers. Like the Apostle Paul, he is a man of purpose, faith,
patience, endurance, and love, even while suffering awful persecution.
Life for him is not a transient waste. It is a stepping-stone to the throne
of heavenly victory. With Paul, the most important man in all the world
can close his eyes to this existence with tranquility. As a valiant warrior,
victorious after the siege, the most important man in all the world can
testify:

As for me, my life is already being poured away as a libation, and the
time has come for me to be gone. I have fought the good fight to the
end; I have run the race to the finish; I have kept the faith; all there is
to come now is the crown of righteousness reserved for me, which the

Lord, the righteous judge, will give to me on that Day; and not only to me but to all those who have longed for His Appearing. The Lord will rescue me from all evil attempts on me, and bring me safely to His kingdom. To Him be glory for ever and ever. Amen. (2 Tim. 4:6–8,18)

8.
The Nobility of Womanhood

Beauty without virtue is like a
flower without perfume.

The finest legacy that could ever be gifted to mankind is the person of a WOMAN—Woman of Devotion, Woman of Sacrifice, Woman of Love. Nothing else in all the world magnetizes a man's attention as do these exceptional characteristics in a woman.

A man is afraid to die; but a woman is afraid not to live. To a man life may be very personal; to a woman it is usually other-directed. This flows from her natural reception of grace, and her natural outpouring for life. She, for happiness's sake, is compelled to go beyond herself for another. Another's rejection of her giving is her very destruction. If dispirited by such rejection, she must, for survival's sake, find means and ways to "self emerge," regain her sense of adequacy. Bubbling within these God-created females rumble the fires of love to be born—a love for God encompassing a woman's whole heart and soul, her whole mind and strength; and then a love that goes forth to radiate to her whole world.

Christian feminism came forth with the advent of Christianity. In Christianity a woman received her authentic position beside man. This was completely opposed to the inferior status imposed by the Greek society. In Greek civilization, between the fifth to the fourth centuries B.C. (which was one of the greatest civilizations in human history because of its wonderful drama, sculpture, philosophy, art, architecture, political policies, and so forth), a tremendous change occurred after only a few generations of prosperity. It has been noted by historians that one of the outstanding causes was the degraded position of women. History also shows that the so-called cultured woman of Greece held a very inferior status. She was exploited as being a whimsical creature. Her position was to remain in the enclosure of the home.

On the other hand, there is the Roman culture. At one time the Roman lady was considered dignified—refined, cultured, and educated. Later, however, a change occurred in the Roman way of life. Women desired to shine in public and even entered into the arena of sports as coach drivers. Even public gladiatorial combats witnessed Roman women participating. However, all this had a very bad effect on Roman married life. As a result, the old domestic virtues were shattered, and then disappeared. Divorce increased and with it came moral decay.

Christianity, however, gave rebirth to the dignity of women as it openly declared a woman's true strength and virtue over and against the false position assumed by the women of imperial Rome. Christianity fosters a woman's strength and freedom, based upon genuine Christlike charity and chastity.

Such a woman presents herself as a model of godliness, a model of interior perfection. This commands awe and respect from men to the extent of wielding a powerful spiritual and moral persuasion. And the truth of the matter is that such a woman, remaining true to the ideals of Christian womanhood, will never lose her influence over men.

In our contemporary culture, many women have risen, and rightly so, to positions of prominence. Our culture, both here and abroad, has been enriched by women's productiveness and performance. To observe women today is very encouraging. Women have unparalleled opportunities to fulfill their fondest dreams. A woman can venture to the moon; she can successfully run for public office and do an equally good job as do others who manifest virile tenacity. A woman keeps her promises! Theater and film success are within her reach; editorial accomplishment through discriminating literary ability is hers—and a host of many other accomplishments in all kinds of endeavors. Women are coming into their own. Even the sky is no longer the limit.

But whether a woman's plans are to focus on the high and the mighty or on family life, her understanding of herself as a *woman,* made by God, called by God, and sustained by God's Divine Providence, is very important as she determines her life plans. Before she can become anything else, and be successful at it, she must come to grips with her womanhood, in all its phases of transience and change. Becoming a woman is the most important job of her existence. Success at and joy in her vocation or avocation solely derive from this one fact of knowing who she is as a woman of the Creator.

The road to womanhood, however, is not always easy: it isn't always smooth, straight, or unencumbered. Difficulties are inevitable both from within her own self and from forces outside: persons, places, things, situations, and problems. Pain of all sorts may assail her. It may serve more as a hindrance than as any invisible blessing. The dangerous trap here is that a woman might begin to think in terms of despair. She entertains self-doubt about her whole person, body, spirit, and soul. With the onslaught of the natural changes of mood and emotion that come with age, she suddenly realizes as never before that it is not a little girl who lives, but a woman. And she must then ask the basic question: "WHAT KIND OF WOMAN?"

The single answer to this lifetime question rests in the wisdom of great men and women of the past who have counseled with the voice of Socrates: KNOW THYSELF. In essence this means that you need time to stop and to reevaluate yourself holistically—to find out what you believe, what kind of life you really wish to live, what your capacities, strengths, virtues are, what your weaknesses are and how you can utilize them for betterment, what you love and what you hate. Perhaps, the first step is to know that before you come to grips with your personality expression you must realize that you are an individual, a private person. If you answer these questions realistically and honestly, you will be surprised to discover your adult personality. You will be able to solve the mystery of yourself. You will conquer the most difficult world of discovery—*your* world!

Regardless of tedium or age, regardless of occupation, every woman will do what she must with lots of love. Women are people. They have the "stuff" it takes for heroism, a remarkable force that at times gives men positive examples. One cannot help but admire the role of woman in a redeeming Church. Her prayer-filled union with God brings her into contact with her self. Her Christian behavior elevates her as the "restorer of honor, family, and society."

WOMAN OF SACRIFICE

The Church perceives woman moving along the earth, being interested in the touch of the "here and now." With a natural sense, a woman feels deeply with a sick child, with a neighbor who may be living in loss of husband or wife, child or relative, material poverty, or other distress. A woman's *whole being* is involved in such situations. Her spontaneous emotions of love and concern, tenderness and compassion, drive her on a torch-bearing campaign for human care and development. At first, being truly a woman, she moves with the heart. After she satisfies the heart's release, her heart then surrenders to her mind. She innately thinks in terms of hospitals, schools, playgrounds, children's villages. Conscious of her "need" for a power far beyond herself, she humbly turns in prayer to her God.

A dedicated Christian woman, or a woman consecrated with religious vows, soaked by God's grace, directed by His inspiration, can do great things for the people of the Lord. Her essential mission in the world is to be for mankind a living example of total dedication to God. She helps to lead society Godward by her direct and unreserved labors for human causes. The Church has identified woman as the cradle of society. After commissioning her as such, the Church looks to the woman to become evermore the heart of the world. It cannot but be noted that she, the woman of God, is a guardian of decency and upholder of morality. In her quest for restoration of society, she will first recognize social and material needs. In the long run, however, she will look for deeper answers. She will demonstrate absolute faith in Him who came to bring righteousness, renewal, restoration, and harmony of order. She, like all women, will endeavor to eradicate the harm being done by evil-minded people. Her sense of morality, her basic tenderness will reach out to the poor and oppressed. And her natural sensitivity will prompt her to expose the evils of injustice everywhere.

If such a woman's spirit of sacrifice is not placed under the microscope of retreat and prayer, her demonstrations of self-surrendering service will be vague. Her values will be distorted. And eventually, her spirit of sacrifice will consume itself. But if "sacrifice" has an innate power for productivity, when posited in the right environment it can give birth to a hopeful tomorrow.

If there is any quality our contemporary age lacks, it is that which might be called "teachableness," or what St. Thomas called "docility." God wishes to teach us about Himself through His creatures, His creations. God will allow us to grow to our full stature if we allow Him to fill us with knowledge and wisdom. Truth is not only found in the halls of study; it is close at hand in our fellow human beings.

History records the influence of woman as a remarkable expression of the "spirit of sacrifice." The student enjoys reading historical accounts of the achievements of Joan of Arc, Esther and Ruth of Old Testament times, Cleopatra of Egypt, Spain's Queen Isabella, Mary Queen of Scots, and Queen Victoria. The Church itself has elevated to sanctity such great souls as Agnes, Bridget, Teresa of Avila, Margaret Mary, Thérèse the Little Flower, Bernadette of Lourdes, Maria Goretti, and hosts of others.

There are many applications of sacrifice, but all share a common denominator: the forfeiture of something highly valued—an idea, object, or friendship—as proof of a higher love. That is both noble and ennobling. Stripped of fame and honor, riches and property, we are left with only our selves and our God.

WOMAN OF THE LORD: A CALL TO HOLINESS

God's woman is a giver, not a taker. She is not just an onlooker on life. On the contrary, she is always in the middle of life. She cares! She belongs to the moment she is in. Her special knack is in discovering what is worthwhile in another person. Her sense of serenity flows from the truth of her personal security; her joys are inward. She has a satisfying existence in her own mind and imagination. She is needed; and because of this, she has integrity. When she possesses integrity, she lives without the *flaws of sin.* This gives her a wonderful simplicity. It protects her. *She remains feminine,* without forfeiting self-worth.

I have written to this extent on the subject of womanhood for no other reason than to elevate all our minds—but especially the minds of women —to their glorious dignity. May the woman of today be a living reflection and example of the "new Eve" in God's creation: the Virgin of Nazareth.

It is sad that today, in many areas of the media, we are still presented with a negative, shallow image of womanhood. To some people, the "greathearted woman" no longer walks the earth. A satisfying consolation blankets people when they know that a tender feminine hand is there healing, teaching, relieving distress.

Christ left us an example; we should follow in His steps. If we follow Him, our lives, our homes, our societies will be much better and much more the way God wants them to be. 1 Peter 2:21 tells us "This, in fact, is what you were called to do, because Christ suffered for you and left an example for you to follow the way he took."

Not too long ago I remember reading an article about a world-famous surgeon and scientist. He looked over the state of the world, analyzed it as best he could, then publicly made his statement that the modern day's decadence was due to the loss of the sense of holiness. It seemed a strange indictment, all the more shocking to hear from a scientist.

Another magazine writer was curious to discover what this statement really meant. Studying it closely, he kept wondering what the doctor meant by this "sense of holiness." He finally concluded that the "sense of holiness" was nothing less than a "sense of the Presence of God." Soon the writer began to pray; he interviewed religious men and women. His conclusion was that this Presence of God must not be, as it seems to be for so many drifting souls, a vague concept of an "unreachable God," safe in His heaven and unmindful of earth. This Presence of God had to be a living God's Presence really existing within us, associated with our daily lives, our families, our work, our interactions with friends and foes, with all our neighbors whoever and whatever they might be.

PRESENCE! That word bears tremendous profundity connoting not only great knowledge and intense depth, but the power of a person being physically present—as one might say, "We need her presence at the meeting." It may also indicate the very place where a certain person is to be found, as for example "in the king's presence."

When our lives are exposed to the presence of another human being, that person's presence puts us on our conscious best behavior. We behave in the way we think is most appropriate, most dignified, to be accepted and appreciated. The question at hand is, if we can act that way in the presence of another human being, then why can't we act that way in a constant manner of being? If we would like to be considered and thought of by another in a certain way, then why don't we be that way with *ourselves* and be *constant* in that manner of presence?

There are schools of psychology that tell us that all human beings act in one of three ways, according to *how we see ourselves, how we think we would like to be,* and *how we think the world pictures us.* Wouldn't it be wonderful if you and I could combine all three? Well, there is a power to do just that. And that is the Presence of God. Here there is no room for pretenses, but an opportunity for peace and joy, happiness and fulfillment.

When a woman, beautiful and elegant as she is, lives in this Divine Presence, she walks her life's path with heavenly focus: she has her head in the skies and her feet on the ground. That divine influence makes her almost as if she were a Mother of Mankind because she helps God to lead society to Him. The Presence of God in her mind, in her spirit, in her body discloses to others God living in her.

History shows that the nations that survive and prosper are those that manage to keep intact *their sense of holiness.* What, then is at the root of its absence today—especially in our land?

People—whether of Protestant, Catholic, or other faiths—who live a living faith in their God of Heaven cannot isolate themselves from the society in which they live. God wants everything best for us, for our use, to appreciate Him and to advance His Glory. If we keep His presence before us, we will give Him the Glory, and He in turn will give us the power.

The family is so important to God. Its depersonalization destroys society. The woman is the heart of the family. Its moral health depends immensely upon her. When a woman loses her sense of holiness, there comes a steady breakdown in the entire moral structure. Life as a whole loses its holiness and then its purpose.

If the woman is conscious of her God being in love with her, she will respond to God's sense of presence. With God at her side she will be one of the most powerful natural means of bringing healing and restoration to the souls of men; she becomes a living "point of contact" between God's grace and the person in need of this contact. As already pointed out, a successful key to that contact will be her *life of sacrifice*.

I earnestly believe that the Presence of God has not been lost. I think that many men and women have been so distracted by the glitter of contemporary life that they have unconsciously and unknowingly stifled that Presence. Nonetheless, a sense of holiness does permeate every woman. It is part of her very makeup. If she surrenders unconditionally to God's call, she becomes the Good Christian Woman, a natural sacrament in the world. If a woman refuses and rejects this innate gift, then she will become frustrated, disturbed, and selfish. But such women, too, are precious. They too have cost God something. They too are being called to a plateau of sanctity, to sacrifice, to the Presence of God. Let us speak up and offer hope to them.

It cannot be emphasized enough that if a woman loses or suppresses her sense of holiness, she will automatically lose her sense of sacrifice. In any love relationship sacrifice is the only foundation. Love cannot survive without it.

The woman of the Lord, then, has a serious mission to accomplish: the restoration of holiness and sacrifice. With Christ at her side, as He was with His first apostles and evangelists, as He was with Mary of Magdala who went forth and told of His Risen Presence, let the Woman of God play her historical role. Let her be God's natural instrument of influencing the world with the ideals of Christ. Let each woman, each young lady, each teenage girl, be God's instrument through which Christ and His Church can save our world from the darkness of paganism into which it threatens to plunge.

In the words of the late Pope Paul VI:

Conditions have created the urgent task of reassembling the whole Christian community. Women should be a sure means for accomplishing the task. These women prove themselves not only capable of collaboration in good works, but they are also gifted with the genius for reconstruction . . . and when they set an objective for themselves they know how to achieve it.

9.
When We Believe in Youth

Today more than ever before both God and His people, both Church and State have need of young men and women, the youth of society, the fresh arrows for a hopeful better tomorrow, who will go forth valiantly as Christian workers, with a balanced personality, inflamed with prudent zeal, fortified with holy wisdom and truth, powerful with the love of God and man. These young Christian workers are summoned to walk among the giants. They are challenged to march victoriously forward "to heal and to build." Stoutheartedly they cross the lands and seas in discovery: in joy and in sorrow, in success and failure, they give unreservedly "the ingredients of themselves" to build up a world such as God wills it to be: a brotherly society in which the suffering of the lowliest will be shared and relieved by all. (RDO)

Something wonderful happens when a troubled teenager—confused, embittered, disappointed—finds himself or herself. The ice around his or her heart begins to thaw in the comfortable warmth of the love and understanding, the appreciation and the encouragement that a climate of affirmation generates. A new look is born when a teenager, or any human being for that matter, is sincerely acknowledged to be important, to be a somebody, loved primarily by God simply because it is God's trait to love His creatures just as they are. Every adult, religious and lay, professional or nonprofessional, bears the moral responsibility of tapping the spiritual and natural powers of strength that are sleeping dormantly within every young man and adolescent girl. This is affirmation of youth. We as adults are to strive patiently and endlessly to produce a better tomorrow for both Church and state, country and world. We adults of the present, who were the youth of yesterday, must again turn our focus and our endeavors to the youth of all classes living among us. For youth can guide this earthly existence to the destiny of God's joyful creation, or to the devastation of Satan's domain.

The world-renowned Father Flanagan of Boys Town, Nebraska,

proved universally that THERE IS NO BAD BOY, NO BAD YOUTH. Through long and hard years of dedication to that truth, through countless experiences of interpersonal relationships with would-be gangsters, through prayer and wisdom, understanding and love, Father Flanagan proved beyond all doubt that a wayward teenager could "hitch his own wagon" to the giants of the world. Perhaps we adults could understand the secret of his success by knowing as he did that God made all things good; and that any evil ensuing from His creatures stems simply from the lack of some other human to care enough, to touch enough.

It is a principle of life that if two people are to assist and enrich each other, if each is to interpret the other's thoughts, emotions, moods, sufferings, joys, and sorrows, each one must unite with the other in a common denominator of compassion. This in turn engenders love. Love is the great giant maker. Like a piercing arrow, it strikes directly, accurately into the heart of human truth. Love alone grasps the truth when the human mind, despite all its splendid capacity, fails to find the "real." So many of our efforts to understand the growth of youth and what matters to them remain utterly void, blind, unfulfilled. We need to be reminded that love bursts all barriers; it also sees the meaning of a thing.

There is a story about a young artist who brought a painting of Jesus to Doré. He sought from Doré a sign of affirmation of a "job well done." Doré, as was his custom when discerning such things, was slow to answer —in fact even slower than he was prone to be. At last he did respond, with one emphatic statement: "YOU DON'T LOVE JESUS. IF YOU DID, YOU WOULD PAINT HIM BETTER!"

We can neither understand the volcanic eruptions of adolescence nor help and direct this emerging generation to understand themselves, unless we—you and I—take our hearts and minds and forge them into the power of compassion, into the power of love, into the POWER OF GOD'S LOVE PLAN.

As we offer compassion, we offer the meaning of love. When we offer love, we offer the presence of the Creator of Love; we offer His presence of "holy sacrifice." Without love there is no sacrifice; without sacrifice, there is no survival. Our youth are capable of love; and within their very depths dwells bursting energy, a capacity for dedication and commitment. With a worthwhile goal before them, this youth of today, as were teens of the past, are ready for a new birth in life. With existing strength, touched and guided by human concern, graced by the Divine, the adolescents of today will launch out into deeper waters of discovery; and their self-betterment will become the betterment and enrichment of God's plan in this country.

Every human being is called, summoned, to walk among the giants. If one would enter one's own soul, he or she would undoubtedly discover a latent potential slumbering there, waiting for resurrection into "greatness." Like smoldering ashes that slowly simmer into death, the human heart of adolescence needs only the cautious, tender hand of a wise and mature adult. With such stroking, a sympathetic loving adult can transform an otherwise inactive spark into a luminous flame. Such illumination opens *new horizons.* The youth, under such influence and with proper affirmation, can ignite the whole world with a TORCH OF NEW LIGHT.

It might be encouraging to many dismayed and doubtful adults who worry about the state of our world, and particularly about youngsters, to remember that today's problems are not new problems. In 1961 the United Features Syndicate, Inc. ran an article in the New York *Post,* entitled "What Is the World Coming to?" by Eleanor Roosevelt, in which she quoted these passages from a book *Personality and Adjustment* by W. L. Patty and Louise Snyder Johnson:

> Our earth is degenerate in these latter days; bribery and corruption are common; children no longer obey their parents; the end of the world is evidently approaching.
>
> Children now love luxury; they have bad manners, contempt for authority. Children no longer obey their parents; they are now tyrants, not servants of their households. They contradict their parents, chatter before company, gobble up dainties at the table, tyrannize their teachers.

In today's world there are no new evils; there are just new persons committing old errors. Some of these evils are only reactions to "resisting, unwanted pain." A lesson to learn well early in life is that everyone, sooner or later, must inevitably experience "growing pains." No person will ever be a stranger to pain. No individual, young or elderly, will not be visited by suffering—physical, mental, or spiritual. Suffering in all its forms, with its hurts, its grief, its trouble, distress, agony, and disorder, leaves its marks on all of us.

That fact notwithstanding, pain can be borne courageously. A characteristic of the human person is the capacity to endure beyond one's own awareness. There seems to dwell within us a potential to endure even more suffering. The value of suffering depends upon its motive. Everybody must go through it; nobody can cast it off upon the shoulders of another, protesting, "LET SOMEBODY ELSE STAND IT!" The truth of the matter is that some people have more to endure than others. And none of us knows the reason why unless it is because suffering has a quality that seems *to forge fine men and women* so that in the end these chosen men and women will do better than the rest of us.

In moments of such pain and embarrassment, one should be with those who suffer. Our presence can serve to heal another human being with the light of TRUTH that leads to LOVE. Without some kind of loving, a man withers like a leaf on a vine. Shepherding a suffering destitute to truth and to love aids that person to abandon hostile reaction, especially violence. Violence is a reaction against a situation that has become intolerable. A friendly fellowship can make one know that he does not suffer alone. That moment of mutual unity in sympathy can enrich the anguishing person to face the truth that being who he or she is might at times require a walk on a moral tightrope. Truth sometimes is painfully wounding. But if pain is received in the spirit of humility, it serves as a pathway to walk among the giants of humanity. If one is molded in "the real good stuff"—that human stuff out of which men and women of character are made—he or she can take any pain right smack on the chin!

In a special way, our youth of today suffer a very distinctive pain. Often it is a product that we adults have molded through passing on our own unresolved problems and doubts. We have molded the clay; we have produced vessels of clay. Yet in that very clay there exists the precious elements for remolding. Isaiah 64:8 depicts such a process: "And yet, Yahweh, you are Our Father; we the clay, you the potter, we are all the work of your hand."

In every community we find adolescents who are victims of broken homes, the death or desertion of a parent, the presence of a mentally ill parent, or a deep-seated parental conflict. Such troubled teenagers need very special help to conquer the handicaps of self-doubt, guilt, inferiority, and the fear that disarms them when meeting the challenges of life. Adult wisdom and understanding, together with firmness and love, influence and inspire youngsters to gain perspective on emotionally charged problems.

Nobody has the right to demean a youth; in fact, nobody should belittle any other human. Each person is unique: one of a kind. Every individual is of infinite value both to God and to others. Everyone is created in

God's likeness; and everyone is loved in spite of his or her faults. God Himself accepts each and every one of us because of His Creation and through His redemption. God loves each and every one of us; and He loves us just as we are regardless of what time, circumstances, and conditions have made of us.

We adults can perceive in each teenager someone who matters tremendously. Beneath the cute "dungaree doll," the studied rebel, or the deafened waif, we can sense a love that is held captive. Indwelling, just waiting anxiously to spring forth into bloom, reposes an embryo of human life. And on us who have weathered our own human storms, through the wisdom of our own sensitivities, there falls the task of enkindling the spark of spirited love. In the same process, the emerging self recognizes in its own human soul the beauty of God's image.

We adults should aspire to make the world a better place in which to live, pray, and work for the purpose that our youth will one day find their right ideals *in the love of country* and *in the love of God.* Particularly should we stress the latter because practice of religion will fructify human sacrifices through Divine Grace. Without this Divine Benediction, human reason and egotism will dominate the deeper self, thus preventing the best in youth from surfacing.

We elders should not be too critical of youths, especially when they appear to rebel against us. If one would objectively analyze the situation or problem at hand, one would readily see that the youth of today *are not* in rebellion. They are not against restraint; but what they really resent is their elders' not giving them an honorable goal and purpose in life. Consciously our youth do not grasp why they possibly "hate" their parents, why they defy authority, why delinquency so easily controls them. But like a submarine beneath treacherous waters there lurk many questions to solve, anger that is boiling with record-breaking temperatures. What festers deep within these youth is the unconscious protest against a society that has neglected to provide a pattern of high-principled life.

Most of what we teach our youth is taught by indirection. They become anxious, subject to fleeting emotions, like chameleons that camouflage themselves with the colors of the objects upon which they place themselves. Heroes and saints, bandits or sheriffs, motivate young people to a self-destructive imitation. Youth are in search of acceptance. They vitally need affirmation. They learn more by imitation than by absorbing conscious instruction. Young children learn English or a foreign tongue because they hear their parents or their relatives or their teachers speaking it. They would speak French or German or Chinese just as naturally as English if in the crib they were addressed in one of those languages. THEY LISTEN AND THEY IMITATE.

Watch your children at play and you will see at once how they imitate your behavior. A little girl, putting her doll to bed, will say: "You get to bed and stay there. I don't want to hear another word from you." In playing house, children faithfully portray their parents. They observe— and repeat—both their parents' good qualities and their faults. Through such imitation, they find a powerful driving force for their own development. Our children, our youth often put us on a pedestal. They pay us tribute. Unconsciously, in order to somehow resolve their own insecurity, their own need for recognition, they want to be what we are. They are pitifully weak and insecure in their early years. They borrow freely from us, assuming simply that what we do *must be right!* So they speak as we speak and do as we do.

Observe the awe with which little children behold us; they solemnize our every word and action. The big ears of children, for example, listen to our conversation even when we think they are not listening. And before we know it, they are saying what we said, and in the same manner, with the same inflections, same expressions. They absorb our attitudes toward life, and if life for us is a burden of regret, it will be so for them too. But if life for us is something thrilling, an adventure with God at the heart and center, then life will be so for them as well.

It is for this reason that we who are privileged by God's Providence to be parents, leaders of education, ministers of religion, or counselors of youth should embark conscientiously as responsible helmsmen who chart the proper course, who create the kinds of energy necessary for wholesome human maturation.

In sum, we adults should believe in youth! Youth is God's precious treasure. Jesus believed in youth. When He came across young lives both His words and His presence somehow instilled the Holy Spirit's breath of hope, confidence, joy, and challenge. Jesus offered Himself as the source and end of all youth's desires and activities. He alone offered them strength to carry the burden of their pain and sorrow from a Good Friday to an Easter Sunday: from a death to a resurrection. He alone would crown their struggles with joy and success. And when young men or young women have this religious experience, they will definitely show that they are capable of tremendous responsibilities. In love and trust they experience as they had never before the true freedom of Christian

Liberation. What more electrifying charge can young men or women have than to know that Christ, the Son of God, the Galilean of Palestine, loves them, accepts them, calls them, empowers them, and sends them forth as His ambassadors to change the world and not to be changed by it.

10.
Youth and the Challenges of Life

A PRAYER FOR YOUTH

Help me to be a sport in this little game of life. I don't ask for any place in the lineup; play me where you need me. I only ask for the stuff to give You a hundred percent of what I've got. If all the hard drives come my way, I thank You for the compliment. Help me to remember that You won't let anything come that You and I together can't handle. And help me to take the bad breaks as part of the game. Help me. Help make me thankful for them.

And, God, help me always to play square no matter what the other players do. Help me to come clean. Help me to see that often the best part of the game is helping other guys. Help me to be a "regular fellow" with the other players. And, God, if fate brings any misfortunes my way, help me always to take part in the game. Help me never to make up excuses or to say that I had a raw deal. And when the final bell rings, I'd only like to know that You feel I've been a good kid.

Finally, God, help me never to go astray; keep me in your protection. And if I'm ever in trouble, keep me on the "up and up" and, God, I want to thank you for everything that I have received in the past or anything that I may get in the future, because I know everything comes forth from You to me, God. (RDO)

To confront that challenge gallantly, one must possess an abundance of resources. The business of life is to live and to live well, and adequately and abundantly. Reverend E. Stanley Jones, a famed missionary who spent many years in China, once stated that everyone may and can live abundantly. He also stated that this age knows almost everything about life except how to live it. As we consider these statements, both you and I realize that it is not enough to know about life—we must know how to live it.

A student who leaves the discipline of science sooner or later must face the challenges of life. Relying solely on his previous academic resources, the young adult immediately begins to pick life to pieces. He begins to examine its constituent parts and then fails miserably to put it together again. He spends long hours on analysis; but he falls short in synthesis. In his attempt to dissect life, he has desiccated it in the process. Overwhelmed by human influence, with science at its peak of discovery, the young adult suddenly loses his contact with the spiritual. Enmeshed in scientific pursuits, God appears as a stranger to him. Sooner or later, the young adult loses his way along the pilgrimage of life. Christianity seems farfetched; it no longer focuses the young adult's vision upon who he is, where he is going, and who his God is. Sooner or later, overpowered by the human need to survive, consumed in error and egotism, the young adult becomes a prey to the onslaughts of mental and spiritual sickness. In ignorance, he has abandoned sanctity and morality. That can be so sad. But in God's Divine Providence, these slips can be corrected by re-inviting the Lord's abundant grace into his life.

To the young people of the world, I say:

YOU ARE IMPORTANT!

YOU ARE SOMEBODY!

YOU ARE UNIQUE!

YOU ARE ONE OF A KIND!

GOD MADE YOU AS A MOST PRECIOUS TREASURE!

GOD CREATED YOU IN HIS LIKENESS!

GOD MADE YOU WITH INFINITE VALUE!

GOD LOVES YOU!

GOD ESTEEMS YOU EVEN IN YOUR FAULTS!

JESUS CHRIST, THE SON OF GOD, CAME TO EARTH TO SAVE YOU!

JESUS CHRIST, THE SON OF GOD, CAME HERE BECAUSE HE LOVES YOU!

JESUS CHRIST COMES TO GIVE YOU A SENSE OF REALITY!

JESUS CHRIST CONSIDERS YOU THE HOPE OF THE WORLD!

JESUS CHRIST CALLS YOU TO EXPERIENCE HIS PRESENCE!

JESUS CHRIST SUMMONS YOU TO BEAR HIM IN YOUR HEART!

JESUS CHRIST ASKS YOU TO REALIZE THE HOPE THAT IS IN YOU!

Young people, the Master asks you to:

be rooted in faith . . .

give spiritual value to your actions . . .
be bearers of hope . . .
bring Christian joy to all . . .
be dynamic witnesses to the Easter message . . .
be disciples of love . . .
be the sign of Christ . . .
be worthy . . .
dream of a new world . . .
. . . society is waiting for you . . .
. . . Christ is waiting for you . . .
be open to grace . . .
open your hearts to Christ . . .
. . . Christianity crowns your personality . . .
. . . Christ alone is your way, your truth, your life . . .
call others to discover Christian joy . . .
let your actions mirror your soul . . .

11.
A Talk with Youth

Dear Young Men and Young Women:

You are men and women of God. You will never be able to run away from this truth. But what a wonderful truth it is. All your uniqueness comes from the fact that God loves you, God made you, and God wants to be your intimate companion. Another word of encouragement is that in spite of our moments of human weakness, our moments of ignorance, our frailties, our wild passion, God is always ready to pick us up and to love us all the more. And if we give Him that chance, He strengthens us with better power, a power that worldly-minded people can't understand.

I'd like to take this opportunity to speak to you directly. Consider this short chapter as a "heart-to-heart" talk—and then use it for reflection. Since you cannot be physically present to share conversation with me, I must do this through the written word. Perhaps we can make this a journey together, something like the *Pilgrim's Progress*. We might meet some pro's and con's along the way. But I promise you, every way will be one of positive consideration, affirmative recognition of your worth, and honest guidance to make you be what you really are: important, unique, one of a kind, somebody, a child of a rich heavenly Father! Will you give me this joy to serve you?

When I was a young priest twenty-seven years ago, I worked with all sorts of teenagers. Some were would-be gangsters squandering their precious lives along the Chicago streets. Yet somehow with God's grace I was able to draw them from the streets to me. Of course I had to offer a lot of attractions like teenage clubs, a clubhouse, pool tables, Ping-Pong tables, jukeboxes, and many other exciting things. But being a priest, as I suppose you can realize, I used these things only as a means to draw these youth to the reality and beauty of who each one was, and to draw them to God. It was surprising how much each one of us grew better through this. I myself learned a lot from those youngsters; and, in turn, I passed on to them whatever good I had accumulated through my life and my studies. The beauty of it all was that it worked. And a lot of those kids eventually became good men and fine women. A few became doctors and lawyers. A few others went off to study to be priests. Some joined the service—and a few did not come back from war. They were killed trying to make this country, this world of yours and mine a better place to live. Sometimes I wonder if it was all a waste. But then I go to the chapel and pray. Other times I just stop and think. When I do, I remember a priest/army chaplain who attended a young soldier, once my altar boy at Santa Maria Addolorata Church in Chicago, who was mortally wounded on the battlefield. As he was dying, he told the priest to get a message back to "Father Ralph." "Tell Father Ralph, thanks for giving me the break he did. Tell him to tell my mom that I made my confession with you right now. Tell him that I received my commun . . . ion. . . ." As he was finishing this sentence, my former altar boy went home—a real hero for God and country. Sacrifice always pays off in the long run, doesn't it?

Somewhere along the years of my early priesthood I came across these written lines: "EXPERIENCE TEACHES US THAT LOVE DOES NOT CONSIST IN LOOKING ANOTHER IN THE EYE: BUT RATHER THAT IT IS LOOKING OUTWARD TOGETHER IN THE SAME DIRECTION." And so, I'd like to make this a chance to look outward in the same direction with you. I invite you to jot down your reflections and thoughts on a piece of paper. Make it your personal diary. Keep it secret; keep it between you and God. Perhaps we could start off with a special prayer. The prayer is simple and in the first person. It is your prayer; it is just for you.

Dear God, give me what it takes to be a holy youth! Give me courage to do what is hard; courage to say NO to sin; courage to hold off the quitter in me. Lord, give me a clean mind and clean speech; let me have clean eyes and clean hands. Help me to cherish cleanliness, and to recognize that it brings happiness. Let me appreciate that in purity all things have value.

Dear God, give me the gift of kindness, so I may never hurt another youth. Teach me to control my temper and my tongue, so that they do not become the instruments of cruelty. I know my own importance, Lord, but let me never fail to see that others have importance too.

Grant me strength of spirit to defeat self-pity. If at times I am lonesome, lead me to the knowledge that to be loved I must be lovable; that I will have no real friends until I earn them.

Dear Father in heaven, sometimes it is hard for me to talk to you.

I've been a stranger to prayer. But please listen to me. Grant me the bigness I sincerely need to be cheerfully obedient. Remove from my personality a sullen spirit. Teach me to take orders, so that some day I will know how to give them reasonably to others.

Grant me zest and drive to conquer laziness. Never let me feel that I can be served without serving, or get without giving. Instruct my young tender heart in the love of work, so that I may know the joy of rest.

Dearest Father in heaven, grant that I may long only for you; that I may surrender all other loves for your sake; that I may surrender any dependencies and addictions to you; and in the paradox of surrendering them to you, because of my love for you, I will be able to learn to love everything with you, for you, and through you.

Grant me the most precious of gifts: that of being able to discern good from evil. May I walk in peace of mind which comes from knowing that I will never lead another to sin. By your grace, may no one be cheapened because he or she kept my company. Let all who love me learn to love you more! And finally, dear Lord, give me such brightness, laughter, and grace that you will find in me a temple for your Holy Spirit. So, dear Lord, come into my heart; come to me just as I am. Be my Savior; Be my Lord!

As you made this prayer, I could not help but think how God was calling you to have the religious experience of Himself. And as you turned to Him, you must have been convinced that He alone can strengthen you! It is Christ alone who can meet your needs. He alone can wipe away your tears! Christ alone can comfort your young wounds, your human hurts! Christ alone is the one who can make your life cleansed. And He alone can be the one to give you a new start, new power for greater service. May your life be strengthened in the commitment you just made!

God is calling you first to know yourself; second to accept yourself; third to share yourself with others. A very important truth to remember is that you are men and women of God! Since God created you in His image, you should go forth into your daily encounters with your actions reflecting the God in your soul. If you are determined to do this, you will decide once and for all to live authentic Christian lives!

As you look out upon the vast world which enfolds much beauty, you will become awed. Tremendous indeed are your responsibilities. Tremendous goals are in front of you. Forward you must go, with all your strengths, integrating your physical gifts with your spiritual ones. As you look out upon the world that summons you, try to realize the hope of mankind that is in you. As you dream of a better world, you yourselves must become that better world. You are destined to make your life and that of others fulfilling. Do your best! Take advantage of the short adolescent years allotted to you. Utilize your adolescence; develop your growing years. Mature yourselves in studies that are sound and sensitive to the needs of your world. Fortify your soul with the power of prayer. And in so doing, you will bear before your eyes the truth that the ultimate cause of all creation is not man, but God.

As you attempt to contribute yourself as a gift to the world, make your gift a dream come true. Work arduously for a better tomorrow. Let your realistic endeavors materialize. With God in your minds, with love in your hearts, with zeal in your spirits, with prudence in your outlooks, go forth to balance those marvelous moments of enthusiasm with those difficult moments that arise either within yourself or from others.

Time passes very rapidly! Soon indeed, in fact very quickly, the years of adolescence are gone! Arduous as the year's study may be, all too soon comes the day of graduation. All too soon the young men and young women of academics become the young men and young women of careers. As you leave the halls of studies—hopeful, enterprising, desirous of success—go forth as another class to leave its beneficial mark upon the pages of history. Let not your class be listed as only another group leaving the portals of college or university. But conscientiously *walk into manhood and womanhood.*

It is not an easy world that awaits you. You will meet the coddled, the weak, the doubting. But with God in your hearts and knowledge in your mind, you will survive; and great will be the honor you shall win. You must be such! You must realize that the inheritance of your generation is toil and sweat, tears and sorrow. But you must also know that out of the bitterest battle the sweetest victory is won.

I, as a servant of God speaking to you in this way, really envy you! Why? Because within your lives rest the power and the glory of solving the problems you will meet. These tasks that you as youth will meet today are for GIANTS! If you remain staunch in your faith, YOU WILL WALK AMONG THEM!

God Bless You.

12.
Called to Arms

A long time ago, St. Ignatius of Antioch said: "Now I begin to be Christ's disciple." By that, Ignatius meant that he wanted to direct his every intention, his every action, and each operation to the praise and service of his Almighty Creator. He recognized that as God supplies the power to each human being, each in turn should give the glory to God.

We often hear the popular phrase that all the world loves a lover. Through observation, we perceive that the world not only loves but also needs love: a love that comes through *leaders*. Not only in the present age, but throughout history, we see that the human race is divided into two groups: those who lead and those who follow. What is particularly edifying is that authentic leaders are both wise and humble. They acknowledge that they too in their weak humanity need someone to lead them. Great leaders depend on other great leaders.

Every person at some point in life searches for his or her own "hero." This hero may be real or imagined. But the search is actually for some source of inspiration. To search or wander in this way does not mean we are lost. Nothing great can be accomplished without the inspiration, incentive, and guidance of an *ideal*. We all possess a driving power to pursue some personal ideal. It is interesting to note that no matter how down-to-earth a realist may appear, even a realist clings to his or her ideal. In the mind of a realist, there is always the blueprint, "the perfect image," of what he or she can be or attain.

To be a leader takes a very special quality. A person in leadership is one who is chosen, one called to arms. Whether male or female, young or old, rich or poor, sick or healthy, black or white, the leader is the one who carries himself or herself, people or nation from crisis to conquest. These are extraordinary persons who appear upon the multiple scenes and avenues of life. Their forceful energy is seen in their fiery individual steps trotting valiantly onward, forward. They promptly and boldly take command. They know how to deal positively with a threat. From the discipline of their minds they lay down conditions and terms that in the final analysis appeal to all.

All leaders must respond to this call to arms. They must be holistic men and women dedicated to holistic human needs—those of body, spirit, and soul. During the time of their leadership they must enrich the land that belongs to God and is only leased to man. Tragedy will test their staunch, reliable characters. Trials will prove whether the leader possesses the necessary strength of character that leadership demands.

Are you called to be a leader? Remember, you are precious in the eyes of the Lord. You have within yourself "great potentials." God can use you for the building up of mankind. God can use you to help a nation find itself and renew itself. You—just as you are—are more noble and striking in your bearing than you think. You have the power of discipline within you far superior to what you may imagine. You are dynamic! You are courageous! You are strong! You are terrific! And you are intelligent, resolute, and articulate; and as you are thoughtful, kind, and humane, you can go forth as a leader and make this world a better place in which to live. You are called to serve another by the call to arms! God has a plan for this world. God has a plan for you to make His plan a reality. God trusts you. God has confidence in you. If you will only follow, God will lead you to lead.

To follow Christ *without question* is a big challenge. Christ the King and the Leader marches onward as a general would lead his armies. A leader like Christ not only calls you to arms but he leads you, sustains you, battles alongside you against the forces of evil. With Christ in your mind, with love in your will, and zeal in your heart, you enter the arena of life to subdue the wiles and snares that surround our existence. With Christ and the power of His spirit, you battle against the seductions of the flesh and the subtleties of Satan. You will battle against the media's evil promulgations and falsehoods. You will purify, in the light of truth, "half-truths" found on university campuses and in halls of learning. You will redress the distorted images of "real life" presented on TV and in the cinema. Your influence will be not that of a neurotic Christian. Nor will you go forth as a religious fanatic caught up in means and methods and forgetting your goal. Your goal is to help the businessman to be moral in his interpersonal transactions. You positively influence others who have contempt for God, who harbor prejudice, who treat others unjustly. You help others overcome the idolatry of self. Humbly, patiently, carefully, you confront the morally decadent, the drunkard, the sinister pervert, and in the words of Isaiah 40:1: "You give comfort to my people."

As champions of the individual, you begin successfully to rebuild society's rough spots and to restore respect for family life. Your influence on individuals will in turn filter into public life. All our universities will once again become defenders of truth. Relativism in philosophy—the theory that everything changes; pragmatism in politics—that if it works it's right; sentimentalism in religion—it is feelings that are important—will all be upturned. A new vista will emerge, and that vista is Christ's challenge to you. He calls you to capture the mind of every person with His truth, to subdue the heart of everyone with His love.

If you heed Christ's call to arms, your greatest reward in this life and in the next will be knowing that you caused Christ, the Son of God, to reign with His grace in the soul of every person you met.

13.
Before the Altar
I Vow My Love to You

The oldest and most beautiful love story in the Bible is that of Rachel and Jacob. An account of this romance is found in the first book of the Old Testament. Every line unfolds the depths of human desire, human passion, and utmost dedication. But love always costs something if it is to be worthwhile. The price of real love is pain. But then, all pain disappears when real love is the basic core. Jacob experiences this. As a fugitive from his own home, as an outcast from his own land, he comes to a strange territory: to the land of the people of the East. And, as the story unfolds, we see Jacob coming to that "well of sacred wells," that well to become perennially known as "Jacob's Well." There, from his "exiled journey," he finds rest and refreshment. Above all, *there* he finds love.

Rachel, the daughter of Laban, comes to draw water. And as she does, the eyes of the young exiled Jacob fall upon her beauty. He is attracted to her external beauty as a projection of the heavenly Creator's splendor. Inner beauty has a special way—distinctive of itself—to magnetize unto itself. And so it is, right there at that well of ancient time, that two hearts become one in the bonds of mutual esteem and love. Their hearts unite to face life's inevitable human experiences. Yes, they are willing and ready to bear with their own and each other's infirmities, weaknesses, and inadequacies by offering to each other "precious comfort" in sickness, trouble, and sorrow. Love does not abandon itself in spite of the cost. And so, in honesty and industry, both Jacob and Rachel ardently work for each other and provide for each other. In spite of hardships, they recall that "first glance" and are able to encourage each other in things that pertain to the spirit. The longing in their eyes becomes the intent of their wills: they come together as husband and wife and live together as heirs of the grace of life.

Those who are acquainted with this heart-moving love story know the treachery and deception of Laban, Jacob's future father-in-law. Industrious and foxy, cunning and devious, Laban forces on Jacob fourteen years of hard labor and dedicated service before Rachel can be his wife. But ardent love, founded on truth and not on mood, knows by its own fires of devotion how to make calamities serve. Obstacles, no matter what kind, often lead to finding grace. GREAT MOMENTS COME OUT OF DARK PERIODS. The worst of times can bring out the best in us. With the spirit of repentance for past wrong decisions, Jacob sublimates his present misfortune. He makes it spiritually creative. New hope is born. Fourteen years of bondage become his opportunity to grow from the old way into a new way.

It is a time for repentance and reversal. Before God can give Rachel to him, Jacob himself has to tear up his old roots. And his fourteen years of suffering labor are acute. His conscience is cleansed—especially from those things that caused his spiritual and material bankruptcy. Grace finally comes to him in his wounded humanity: the crown of his labors is a "resurrection in joy." He finds new life in the strength of his God, who is calling him to higher things. And Rachel is given to him as a stepping-stone. God uses Jacob's desire for Rachel to teach him, as He teaches all of us, that only when we learn to give out constantly will we be ready to take in constantly. And so, at that moment of renewed life, Jacob says unto Laban: "Give me my wife; for the time has come for me to go to her." And so Laban gathers all the men of the place and gives a feast. Then Laban gives his daughter Rachel in marriage.

What does this love story tell us? Without some kind of loving a man or a woman withers like a leaf on a vine. God led Jacob and Rachel together. In turn, each led the other to the portals of their eternal destinies. God made them recognize love in its perfection and uplifted their minds to the discovery that He is the Author of Love. When they found God as the source of their love, then God was able to share His blessings with them. Jacob also learned another very important truth: *that in life one cannot change things, one can change only one's self!* Jacob learned, as many of us must learn as well, that honor was more important than acquiring success or fame.

The poet was accurate when he stated that *we must love another or die;* we must either do something with love or we must be depersonalized. God used Rachel to influence Jacob to do good. He allowed the beauty of Rachel to bring Jacob to his senses and to know the call of the Lord. When he loved without selfishness, Jacob discovered that Life that dwelt within him. Every journey of personal insight made in truth and in spirit fructifies itself in the life and plans of God. Weaknesses are no longer impediments. God gives birth to our strengths! Rachel trusted Jacob; and

Jacob believed in Rachel's love. And we all know so well that when we trust someone, we bring out the best in that person.

Those who enter into marriage can derive valuable instruction from the above scriptural story. Matrimony is the chosen state for many people. But why is it that after a short period of time, perhaps after the "honeymoon" has worn off, those once exciting church bells stop ringing for some? What about that holy commitment "until death do us part"? It is so unfortunate that so many come to reject and deny that once solemnly pronounced vow. Why does our society—God's people—suffer countless and innumerable marital failures? WHY IS THERE SO MUCH UNHAPPINESS IN MARRIED LIFE?

After twenty-seven years of ministerial work, after so many moments of dedication to healing sessions, I can find only two possible answers. The first might be the fact that probably those who have entered marriage had no real understanding of what it is. And, therefore, their will (their love) had no interpersonal foundation. The gift of marriage is a *person, not a thing!* Many people base their commitment of marriage on romance. Romance of itself can serve a purpose; but in the final analysis, it does not last. It is only a flickering spark of love, a physical attraction, but not dependable. The other possible reason is that perhaps once having entered upon marriage properly, with understanding and verbal commitment, the couple—through time and circumstances, through unforeseen conditions—forgot (or lost sight of) the authentic meaning of love. Somehow, the destitute couple lost the meaning of commitment. They forgot that *nothing worthwhile is ever accomplished in this life without passion; and the basic passion of all is love.* Whoever mocks love outrages human nature. God is love, and whoever embraces love within the context of Christian living will discover God and win the victory of heaven.

Marriage is a vocation and it is lived out to the end in the *expression of love.* The Christian marriage is probably the most romantic story of God, Man, and Woman. The practice of marriage is an art because it is a way of living. Marriage is born of love. And that love is active in all its stages. It continually expresses itself. It is joyful. It is maturing. It is painful. It is productive! Difficulties certainly must come. But they come with purpose. And though there are people who are in difficulty, yet there are those who are happy. People who love each other *together* surmount these hardships. They even see themselves draw closer together because of their problems.

Perhaps we can observe that many marriages fail because of the false concept of the four-letter word "love." How sad that love nowadays is so often nothing more than a lyric in a popular song. As such, it is a tune overplayed! It comes across as something mushy, fleshy, emotional, and sometimes even cheap. Love is too beautiful for that. It was not meant to be degraded. It is too precious. It belongs to persons; it belongs to people.

Today, more than ever before, this precious word, "love," needs to be re-enthroned as queen of all the emotions. The other emotions—hate, sadness and joy, pleasure and pain, fear and boldness, desire and aversion, anger—encircle love; they can protect it or satisfy it. Human love needs to be purified in the alchemy of Divine Love which is its origin. To modern young men or women who are new to their growing experiences, physical attraction, emotion, and passion are frequently confused for love. But in the passing of time what was once exciting later becomes boring. We are left to confront the never-ending philosophical truth: physical attraction can never be the foundation of love. ALL PHYSICAL THINGS BY THEIR VERY NATURE MUST CORRUPT, DECAY, WEAR OFF IN TIME. They must become tiresome, for they are not everlasting. Our own human longings are evidence of this truth. Our spiritual life also proves the words of St. Augustine that our hearts will not rest in peace unless they rest in the Lord.

Rather, we know that love is founded on sacrifice, without which love doesn't exist. Love founded in sacrifice is not only a *call to friendship* and to the interests of the other, but it induces assimilation into the other person. It submits itself unconditionally to the other person's welfare; and in so doing, it requests little or nothing in return.

All things are bearable when there is true love! If the price of love is pain, then it is also a fact that all pain vanishes with *sacrificial love*. A father might work many jobs and spend many hours from early morning to late evening trying to meet the appropriate needs of his wife and children. Love brings his sacrifice to joyful fruition. Many a devoted mother spends endless hours at the bedside of her husband or children when they are ill. Again, this time and energy is a sacrifice of pure love.

Marriage is a covenant between God and two spouses. *God does nothing that He intends to be significant and permanent with humanity without a covenant.* Jesus demonstrated the love of "agape" when He laid down His life for us. A covenant always requires a spirit of sacrifice. Christian marriage is based on that sacrifice of Jesus. By this covenant, therefore, both a man and a woman lay down their lives for each other. The two become one—the beauty of this is that each one lives no longer for his or herself, but spends his or her own life in a *new life* in and through and for the other. This mutual surrender, this mutual expending of the spirit is an earthly covenant until the end.

God cannot be left out of a marriage. He is the bond of love that unites a couple's mutual sacrifice. His presence continues to activate their mutual gift giving. A union like this, approved by God, will result in a couple's knowing each other in a way no other person should be allowed to know either of them.

After the threshold is crossed, the newlyweds leave behind their happy-go-lucky days and begin a new phase in their life. It is one of responsibility from the ground up, from here to God, and a life of interpersonal dedication and service to each other. Proverbs 31:10–31 describes a loving wife encircling all her attention and focus on her husband: ". . . [his] heart has confidence in her. Advantage and not hurt she brings him all the days of her life."

St. Paul renders the husband's feelings. His love is reciprocal. His wife is his glory. She has made him be someone special, important; she has been the inspiration of all that is good in him. And he in return offers her the homage of his devotion: security and covering, protection and provision, love and respect.

I must presume that every couple really does intend that their marriage be a happy and permanent one. But minds and attitudes change in the face of unexpected—and unresolved—difficulties. Somewhere along the road some couples forgot "for better or for worse." Marriage is always for the better as far as God is concerned; but it is for the worse when the couple ignores God's directions in His Divine Love Plan. The signs of rejection are so depersonalizing, so destructive. Love begins to go sour. And the road to hate is paved by indifference. This prompts retaliation expressed by "Indian giving." Slowly, love is taken back; selfishness masters the souls of the couple. And finally, they accuse with contempt: "I would never have married you if I had known you were like this. . . . you, a drunkard, a gambler; you who are so promiscuous; you who seek expressions without love, without commitment. I would never have taken you if I had known how selfish you are! You are so self-centered; you are so 'cheap'; you are a stranger to respect." And so on. No evidence of the spirit of sacrifice there. It's no wonder, then, that love collapses.

Such scenes as this do exist and are replayed every day by countless married partners who avoid or escape their marital commitment. When that spark is snuffed out, then the oblation of love for each other no longer wants to sacrifice either for the other or for their family. They have lost the will to love. And they have substituted for love the false deceptive building up of the ego. As a result, the white house up on the hill now has a "For Rent" sign on it. And a family for God has been destroyed.

How can this awful tragedy be averted? The answer is threefold: you must love your partner as Christ loves His Church; you must love your partner as you love your neighbor (no neighbor is loved more than your partner); and you must love your partner as you must love your enemies (you do this by repenting).

You avoid such destruction in your marriage by practically living with, for, and through each other. In praxis, you both must mature together in the various phases of your years. You seek ways in which you can blend, assimilate, make your lives TOTAL! It is almost like two bodies with one soul. It is all for one and one for all. Moreover, in this process of blending, there is the very important element that is often overlooked, forgotten, or flatly ignored. And that is: YOU BOTH MUST BE MORALLY BENEFICIAL FOR EACH OTHER, and this power will lead you both to God and not to Satan, to heaven and not to hell. Marriage was made in God's mind, and on earth it must benefit your soul.

If a crisis comes along the way, can you remain loyal? Suppose poverty strikes you, sickness threatens your existence, your spouse becomes a drunkard, is unfaithful, violates you. Will you walk out? Hard things to suffer, aren't they? But divorce is not the answer. Divorce is only trying to get even; it is a form of retaliatory equalization. Hurts and wounds are the only products. Healing is very necessary. And that healing can come only through self-honest, sincere *repentance.* The first repentance is to the author of marriage, God, for your having abused His gift of love in marriage. We are all on our way back to God through this life. When you gave yourselves to each other through Holy Contract, you were affirming that fact and acknowledging that through the vocation of marriage you felt that your journey would be more convenient, feasible, and comforting. You were so absolutely sure that such a union would make your salvation more certain, more productive than it would have been outside of marriage.

But it takes so much humility to say that you are sorry; that you respect each other as human persons who are important somebodies. If God can love you, why can't you love each other? You do this by forgiving each other's human foibles. Look at the beautiful possibilities of being human and how to embellish that humanity into God's best. Before self-ishness attacks you, *you attack selfishness!* Selfishness is the greatest ob-stacle to a happy marriage. Strive to nurture harmony in your lives. Seek mutual agreement regarding everything from religion to art, from music to recreation, from reading to conversation. *Work* at everything! Fight and struggle as you have never fought and struggled before *to protect your marriage from shattering.* Positively, work together, struggle to-gether, cry together, laugh together. But, above all, *live together!* Don't allow the fire of holy love to burn out, but keep it as the flame that it is.

At this point, I wish to serve you as God's channel of Divine Healing. True healing comes from God alone. You each are a gift to the other from God. Never spoil the gift! If you want your love to grow, then focus your love on *the person,* as gift. Our relationship with God undergoes the same experience. Through visible signs He draws us. We are excited, overjoyed. We feel affirmed by God Himself! What a gift! At the beginning of our "religious experience" with God, we come to notice that one loves the Almighty only for His gifts or for the emotions He sends us. The Divine Lover treats us like a young fair maiden who is in the rapture of "being courted." But if the gifts and the attention that the gifts symbolize are no longer given in abundance after the actual marriage has occurred, this in no way indicates that love is in decay. It is not necessarily a sign that the husband's love and devotion is less, but it is evidence that love has been founded on more solid ground, that love has begun its voyage of discov-ery into deeper water. The truth of the matter is that the husband's love is greater. Why? Because in this newfound religious experience of love, the husband is now ready beyond all measure *to give himself with uncon-ditional surrender, wholeheartedly!* And it is not the husband's material gifts that the wife actually wants, not his benevolent compliments, nor even the pleasure she derives that fulfills her being. What she wants is that he love her as a person, and that she too is free to love him as a person. And the great thrill of this interpersonal play is that as each one freely gives to the other, each one remains free to grow in the freedom of their mutual love. They neither hurt themselves in their Christian libera-tion, nor jealously interfere with each other's personal growth.

The truth is simply stated: he loves her, and she loves him. The mo-ment the lovers are loved for themselves, then the nature of the gifts cease to matter. The splendor of this dynamic is that God is at work here. It is God who in His purification of our love is withdrawing all sensible gifts because He wants the union between the human soul and His Divine

Being to be more personal and less dependent on the gifts of His generosity alone.

Shall We Pray?

Dear Father in Heaven, we come before you just as we are. We come in the humanity of our brokenness. It is good for us to know that we are broken people. But you will make us whole. Our love is young and tender. It comes from you. We invite you into our marriage. Stay with us, Lord. Without you we will fumble in this journey together. Grant us a true spirit of your love. As we reflect conscientiously, we know so well that it is *the joy of love we want!* O how true it is that JOY IS THE HAPPINESS OF LOVE—A LOVE THAT IS AWARE OF ITS OWN INNER HAPPINESS. Pleasure, we know, comes from without. And it is good too because you made it to be so. But joy, Lord, that is what we want, because joy comes from within our souls; and nobody can take it away. It is within the reach of everyone in the world. If there is sadness in our hearts, Lord, it is because there is not enough love. Help us through our married lives to radiate love so that those who meet us will be influenced by your Holy Spirit of Love dwelling in us. Walk with us through our married days. May our union be a public witness that TO BE LOVED, WE MUST BE LOVABLE: TO BE LOVABLE, WE MUST BE GOOD; TO BE GOOD, WE MUST KNOW GOODNESS; AND TO KNOW GOODNESS IS TO LOVE GOD, AND NEIGHBOR, AND EVERYBODY IN THE WORLD! O Lord, we can learn this only at the feet of your altar where we make our vows, and our vows make us holy.

Amen

PART III
The Value of
Social Leadership

14.
The Permanency
of the "Yes"

When a representative of God stands before the altar and receives a man and a woman's vows, *that* is a great privilege! Many thoughts and images flicker before his mind in reference to the two people standing there before him. Their hearts seem so joy-filled. There seems to be quiet peace in their spirits because of the tremendous responsibility they are mutually *willing* to accept. The minister sees flowers, veils, lace and rice, white wedding cake, rings. He says prayers. Then more lofty thoughts enter him because of the seriousness of the occasion. And he wonders if this apparently happy couple really do understand that their love will encompass obligations, opportunities, privileges, and challenges that their very special marriage will bring with it. In the prayerful heart of the minister he begs the Almighty Creator of this young man and young woman for Divine Assistance, that these two young lovers will build up their existence together using the spiritual and moral resources that will dispose them for full benefit of the sacramental graces that are given to the married.

Because I am a minister of the Word and a priest of the Sacraments I too feel the awesome responsibility of imparting the visible Christ-blessing upon two aspiring hearts as they stand before the altar to pronounce *the permanency of marriage*. The couple has a host of thoughts about this, their special day, as does the minister, the priest, the rabbi. Sacred indeed is marriage; its privileges must not be taken lightly. And so, as I write this chapter, I ask you the reader to allow me to speak *with you*— not as a stranger, or as a third person to your wedding commitment, but as a *friend who serves mankind with love, and as a priest who renders God's healing love.* I thank you for this privilege.

In preparing these thoughts I came upon an article entitled "Instant Secretary." What struck me particularly was the word "instant." We have "instant" everything these modern days: instant food, instant suntan lotions, instant long-distance telephoning, and instant culture, a name sometimes applied to our new whirlwind tours of the world. So, I thought, why not flash those instant reflections and instant replays that have the power to renew, rebuild, revitalize, give *daily new birth* to maturing married couples? So, let me take your hearts and your minds and let's make this journey of recovery by discovery of all the "nice things" you as married people have.

Marriage is too sacred and too beautiful to take lightly. Yet, light-mindedness often camouflages a basic truth. If we stop and *listen,* we cannot help but hear it. For instance, what would you derive from the wit or cynic who defined matrimony as "an institution of learning in which a man loses his bachelor's degree and his wife acquires a master's." Honestly, what does this say to your listening third ear?

At the basis of many cynical remarks about marriage there is always the fact of an individual person wanting to be recognized as a man or woman. This manhood and this womanhood want essentially to be affirmed, as we want to be appreciated for the surrender of our whole self. Nobody wants to be jilted, or above all, duped into love's sacred commitment. That is the most perfidious of human behavior! Marriage is a real love story; and the parts of that story, man and woman, must be put together in and through and for the Creator of the mystery of falling in love.

An overworked businessman came home one night, hoping to read the evening paper in peace and quiet. But his six-year-old son wanted attention. Tearing into small pieces a part of the paper that had a map of the world on one side and the picture of a man on the other side, the father gave it to his son and told him to put it together again. In ten minutes his son returned. The task was complete! Since the boy had no idea of geography, his father wondered how he had done so well so quickly. "All I did, Dad," said the boy, "was to put the man right. When I did that, the world came out right."

Keeping love together will be the biggest job of your married life. Archbishop Sheen used to say that in the true love of married people, it is not so much that two hearts walk side by side through life. Rather that two hearts become *one heart.* How true this is. Your love did not come from yourselves. If it did, then it will disappear because man and woman by their very makeup tend to the exterior. God, however, brings people together—and He does so for a certain purpose.

We can see then that it is God who brings two people together; and that the real story of our life is a love story with God. And as in all love stories, you begin as two individual human beings. You begin falling in love. Suddenly, because of each other, life is more exciting and richer than it ever has been before.

But then, in some love stories, something unforeseen happens. Lovers begin to separate. They feel they do not love each other anymore with the same intensity. And those who observe this course of events suffer with them. Perhaps we who look on can offer something positive to bring them back to their senses, and maybe even *save their love*.

The love stories we like best are those that make us happy, those that bring joy after hardships and tears. We like to see lovers overcome all the barriers that storm against them, that are separating them. We become tearfully happy when lovers rise from brokenness and find each other, *and they love again!*

We cannot speak of love or of lovers unless we speak of God in this love relationship. Without God, the marriage relationship is not complete; an essential part is missing. God's life with us is a love story. Our Father created this world. It is His world, and we belong to Him. He created this world because He is goodness itself, and the world is good. Because of His love He created it, and because of His love He created you both. Through your marriage God lives in you with His Holy Spirit. And as you live that Spirit you will live your marriage out in His Holy Way.

When God calls two people together into marriage, He intends that His Holy Spirit will reign in the couple's hearts, and that the Spirit will raise them to the life of the Blessed Trinity. The vocation of all—both Jew and Gentile—according to St. Paul in his letter to the Ephesians, is *to live in unity*. This is what Jesus won for all of us by His redemptive death. *But this unity must be retained and maintained by a life of love.* Because people, including Christians, come from different walks of life, there is bound to be friction in their daily encounters, their daily living together. Paul offers Christlike virtue as a medicine. He points out that humility, patience, and charity in putting up with the frailties and faults of others is the only essential remedy to keeping Christian unity.

In the psychological gift of *retrospection* each of us can find lost values. By walking our former steps, by talking our walk, we can live again the Holy Spirit that brought us unity. And so, we, like the little boy in our story who put the man together and brought the world out right, can assemble the puzzled broken pieces. It's a good thing to look within our souls, to retrace our steps. It is a necessary part of the voyage of discovery. God is our starting point. Take your Scriptures. Open to Tobias 7:15 in the Apocrypha:

> And so, taking his daughter's right hand and putting it into the right hand of Tobias, he gave them his blessing: "May the God of Abraham, Isaac and Jacob be with you, and himself join you in one, and fulfill his merciful purpose in you." (Knox)

Why did God bring you together? Why did God have an idea to bring the two of you together? God is head over heels in love with you whether or not you love Him in return. God used the prophets of old to tell Israel that no matter how she kept refusing her God, the Almighty Creator's heart ached and suffered with each rejection, with each mistreatment that Israel continued to inflict on people, whenever she would ignore the poor or fail to continue to live in peace. God knows that you and I cannot be won over against our will. It is necessary that human beings freely invite God into His rightful place in our lives. And so God uses people to influence, to inspire one another. God can even use these words, this chapter, to cause you to respond totally to his love and thereby make Christ alive in your married love.

God formed a people and He formed them into a family. To form a family of chosen people, he established marriage. God performed the first marriage in the Garden of Eden. It was God's idea to have the family in the first place. Before there were cities and governments, before written language, nations, temples, churches, there were families. The family is the most important institution in the world. Many today are wringing their hands with fear and insecurity, because far more important than what is happening on Wall Street or what is happening at the United Nations is what is happening to our families. The home is where characters and attitudes are formed, integrity is born, values by which we live are made clear, and lifetime goals are set.

When a beautiful bride walks down the aisle of a church and stands at the altar, it is not uncommon for parents to shed a few tears. These are "happy/sad tears." Happy tears because this is a joyous occasion, a moment in which their daughter or their son radiates contentment and happiness, but sad tears also because the wise hearts of the parents weigh this step with prayerful concern and hope that *all will be well.*

Go back to the very day of your marriage. That time and that moment were all yours. Do you remember? As soon as you crossed that wedding rail, your childhood days were over. Your words of consent through the marriage vows were like the final cutting of the umbilical cord, a total release from the family womb. The parents' task is over. Afterward they can only sit back, watch, hope, and pray that their years of loving concern and careful training have produced a mature man or woman, one capable of returning love as well as receiving it, one able to adjust to the demands of married life, conjugal responsibility.

The wedding ceremony and ritual contain a significant and indicative note of finality for the son or the daughter while they specify a time for independence. The reality of the moment gives birth to a new existence together with another human being in the bonds of love. It means facing life as it is, sharing joys with each other, and sorrows as well. There should be no iota of a thought of turning back, no clinging to childhood or adolescent crutches! To do so in marriage brings misery; and it sows the seed for possible future disaster.

Beautifully written and described in the Old Testament is the story of Isaac taking Rebekah as his wife. He loved her, this devoted one. In accord with her name, she bore him up valiantly. Upon the death of his mother she consoled him. Certainly a wife, without resentment, should be a consolation to her husband in time of trial; and the husband likewise a source of support for his wife in periods of anxiety. Nor does maturing independence as a married couple exclude tender love and care for both sets of parents. A husband was never meant to replace his wife's father; nor should a wife intend to be a substitute for her husband's mother. These two loves are totally different and must never be intertwined. Love for parent, love for partner are both special and unique. No one can take the place of a mother, of a father; nor should anyone be expected to do so. Both loves are good; both are needed; but they are different and must not be confused!

Whenever a couple, deeply in love, asks me to perform their marriage ceremony, I, feeling a sense of responsibility, often share the following insights either through Scripture, word, prayer, or opportunity of the moment. Absorbed in my every gesture, as they perceive the mood I'm attentively setting, they feel peace. They are grateful for the presence of some authoritative figure understanding them and affirming that what they have decided to do is all right. Believe me, for them it is a great feeling! And so, with an understanding and warmth, I begin:

> In a few minutes you two wonderful people will be standing before me, the priest whom you have chosen, before your parents, friends,

and loved ones, to pronounce your major decision. In a minute or so, you will turn to each other; you will face each other; and in that one special glance of the eyes, you will read the depths of your souls. And as you do so, you will hold each other's hands. You will both by sign and by word promise to share your lives together until death.

This is a commitment, a very permanent one. It is a person-to-person surrender to love and honor each other in happy moments as well as in some unfortunate and discontented ones. You will face together some inopportune sensitivities, moments of poverty, and times of plenty. Sickness and disease will not be strangers to your household. Your love for each other will sustain you; it will restore your willpower to rise and be healed. For better or for worse—in sickness and in health —these are serious thoughts, solemn vows.

A young woman, very much involved with a personable man, fixedly *in love with love,* but wondering nonetheless about the correctness of her course, wrote to me: "Pray for me, dear Father. Pray that I won't turn off the light when it comes. I seem to be learning *that love is so painful and absorbing that one can prefer blindness."*

Regardless of how and when we fall in love, falling in love first involves a seeming attraction to the other's external manifestations and appearances. This certainly seems to be psychologically true. And this type of falling in love is beautiful! It is the very beginning of love. But it is only for the moment, an introduction to a deeper understanding of what those externals *really represent.* Time alone will tell! The *good feeling* will either wax strong and age with constancy, or it will become blinded by self-serving love and die.

But there are moments when death comes to married love. It may come gradually or abruptly: as a slow drifting apart or a fast, hurtful breakup. The latter serves as a deceptive mental satisfaction that the love formerly experienced was never authentic. The drifting away process serves as a slow rationalization that what formerly appeared as a "glimmer of heaven" was in truth only an "infatuation," a short-lived "romance." It satisfied the moment of the lonely heart.

But this, thank God, is not always true. For the majority of married couples, love grows. It builds continuously upward, solidifying that initial strong attraction to each other. It develops with each unfolding phase of human existence; deeper and deeper does it place its roots in "good earth." It blossoms strong! It surmounts death. It lives in the victory of life.

The fruits of such a positive love-growth is that in spite of the faults remaining, the couple, nevertheless, comes to accept them as part of the human condition. And though disagreements continue, these are no indication of "rejection" of the other partner. The positive input resolves itself not in the evil of meaningless compromise but in the unison of two working for the common good. Arguments go on, but end with reconciliation. The road at times may even get rocky—and for periods without ceasing the couple may even drift off in different directions. But eventually, they return to each other, and they resume their journey, ultimately realizing that their mutual love has plunged into a new and richer plane.

The wedding ceremony is very impressive as well as meaningful. But even more impressive is the attendance of friends and relatives assembled in the body of the church. It is important to know why we are all there. The answer is simple. Our presence is "intercessory" as it is "self-enriching." All of us who come to a couple's wedding service do so for two reasons. First, we want to pray for these two young aspiring hearts, these two human beings, *that they may sanctify their commitment to each other.* Second, we come together to offer our best wishes *as prayer intercessors.* And in spite of what life may have done to us who are present, or better still, what we have done with life, we ourselves become inspired to love again, to love afresh. As we serve this new couple through our prayers, we too become recipients of grace for a better tomorrow.

As we pray and intercede for the newlyweds, we beseech Almighty God to guard these two people against the moods of a moment that seek to override reason. And so, it is for this reason that the couple takes a *vow.* A vow offers the possibility to control capricious solicitations.

Love never betrays anyone; sometimes people betray love. It is so absolutely necessary that those launching out into the sea of matrimony grasp the fact that, if they establish their pronouncement only upon sex, they will eventually realize that sex necessarily will direct itself to pleasure. It is ego-orientated; it is ego-receptive. Sex does not contain love; but love does contain sex. One is the cause; the other is only a segment of the expression. Without love, sex makes a person look upon another only as an opposite gender. *It is interested only in self!* And that is an atrocity for human relationships, leading inevitably to hate. This love of self enslaves; it is carnal and erotic. The ugliness of it is that after the pleasures have been easily satisfied, there is the temptation to pursue additional, similar pleasure elsewhere.

Love to be genuine needs to go out into benevolence; it needs to be *personal.* Such a love includes the element of sex only as an expression of surrender. Personal love goes out to the other person; in essence, it is based on the *objective value* of another person. We love that person for his or her own being and we love God; He makes that person who and what he or she is. All frustrated people suffer this one anguish as the basic pain in any miserable situation: that they are not accepted as they are. Nor are they affirmed in that splendor of their own importance. What a tragedy to be only used or tolerated! Personal love seeks understanding, upon which it is built. We say to a lover: "I love you because I *know* you. You are beautiful; you are morally upright; you are artistic; you are you, and I love you because you reflect most splendidly all the qualities of your Maker."

This kind of love can exist simultaneously with carnal love, or it can live apart from it. One can be in love without there being physical attraction, as it is also possible to have physical attraction without any love. What every lover demands is the *personal love* in *the other person's will.* It is torture to have only the body from the other partner *without* the surrender of the total person through the will. In personal love there is no possible substitution of a person. *This* person is love, not another!

Love to be supreme needs to be Christ-rooted. Christian love embodies the most comprehensive of all the elements of sex and personal love. We love the other person above all as a child of God redeemed by Christ. For this reason we do not abuse that other person. Christian love seeks no selfish return; it does not even harbor a *hope* of love—or anything else—*as a return.* For a Christian, one sees the other person as one for whom one must sacrifice oneself, not for the selfish gratification of the other's attractiveness, talents, sympathy, and the like, but only because of God. We see a soul to be saved; and in Christian marriage, our relationship to our spouse serves as a stepping-stone for his or her salvation.

The vocation of marriage—and that is what it is, a *vocation*—leads to human fulfillment, and thereupon, to human happiness. This happiness comes through holiness and sanctity; and therefore, requires God as its foundation. God wills two in one flesh: He does not tolerate it; He wills it! Because He wills it, He sanctifies the couple through such physical union. Sexual love contributes to the ascension—the growth—of love.

This sort of love in marriage is matrimony as a sacrament. It is something holy. Its inspiration is Christ.

Marriage as something holy is a symbolic sacrament of the nuptials of Christ and His Church. It is something much, much higher and more significant than just the natural order of a union of man and woman. Being a symbol, it seeks for something concrete by which we in our human understanding can perceive its significance—just as the Cross, for instance, reminds us of the whole mystery of Christ.

Marriage is a union. This union is dramatically as well as romantically expressed by the ring(s) given during the ceremony. It is the outward sign of the marriage vows. A ring on the third finger of the left hand announces to all, in stark unquestionable terms, that the wearer of the ring *belongs* to someone in a holy commitment.

But to the giver and the wearer, the wedding band manifests much more. It carries far deeper implications. It both visibly indicates and reminds the spouses of their promise to love and to be faithful. It proclaims that this man and this woman are set apart as man and woman, as husband and wife. Their existence together is designed by God's love plan. God has come to this wedding and He blesses this love.

And so, God uses signs and symbols in the sacrament of marriage to help us understand that a man and a woman are now joined in a special way.

The concept of *sacrament* is not something added to the nuptials. No! It is something distinctive; it is an *elevation* of that marriage consent and places it in the order of grace. The priest's presence and ministry help bring order to the surrender of man to woman and woman to man. The role of the priest is *to ratify* and *to bestow* the Church's official blessing. In so doing, the Church empowers heaven's benediction upon the man and woman who will procreate new members of the Mystical Body.

And so, we have seen the splendid union of married love. And we can conclude by simply making the analogy that marriage is a "little cameo" reflecting the greater espousal of Christ and His Body, the Church. And to all couples who are beginning a new life, I would like to propose a toast that has been handed down in one family for generations: "May your life be like a beautiful painting with plenty of light and color and just enough shadow to make the painting complete."

15.

In Praise of Motherhood

The most important person on earth is a mother! The late Joseph Cardinal Mindszenty, speaking about his own mother, said that a mother may not be able to lay claim and honor for having built Notre-Dame Cathedral. She need not. She has built something more magnificent than any cathedral—a dwelling for an immortal soul, the tiny perfection of her baby's body. The angels have not been blessed with such a grace. They cannot share in God's creative miracle to bring new saints to Heaven. Only a human mother can. She is very close to God.

Whatever our life conditions may have been, whatever sufferings life's circumstances may have brought, the truth of the matter remains that we are here on this earth because of our mothers. Years may rapidly parade before us, flashing with them many scenes, a lifetime of memories. We recall those many maternal moments of care and devotion, of nurturing hopes and aspirations, of dedicated labor. We can never forget our youthful dreams. It was mother, so precious to us, who encouraged our longings unto attainment. And so, all of us, you and I, must salute our mothers. Let us do so while we have the time. Some of the saddest moments during an inner healing session are when adults emotionally break down in copious tears, recalling words and expressions of love never given to their mothers or to their fathers while they had the opportunity. Sad indeed it is to have a mother and not recognize the splendor of her role to child and child's to mother. But more sorrowful is harboring all those guilt feelings.

Speak your heart while you can. Do something beautiful while you are able. Nobody can take the place of your mother! A great mother is the finest legacy ever granted. She is the best fortune ever to come our way. Would that children would embrace their mothers and know that they are unselfish in their care and devotion. What good mother has not both lived and died with her child? In each phase of growth she watched with enthusiasm as she rendered her sympathetic touch. Midnight vigils are not strangers to her. Her children could not help love her because she in her every thought, word, and deed loved them first. Her love demonstrated itself with her toil. In every hurt she almost died with her child's wounds. How soft were her hands when she stroked our brow, kissed away our pain. No angel voice can compete with her lullabies. No other love is like the love of a mother.

Dale Carnegie in his book *How to Win Friends & Influence People* tells an interesting story that would benefit many of us:

Many years ago a boy of ten was working in a factory in Naples, Italy. He longed to be a singer, but his first teacher discouraged him. "You can't sing," he said. "You haven't any voice at all. It sounds like the wind in the shutter." But his mother, a poor peasant woman, put her arms about him and praised him and told him she knew he could sing, she could already see an improvement, and she went barefoot in order to save money to pay for his music lessons. The peasant mother's praise and encouragement, her sacrifices, changed that boy's life. His name was Enrico Caruso, and he became the greatest and most famous opera singer of his age.

Yes, great indeed is a mother. We see the beauty within her with each birthday, with each Mother's Day. She grows older. There are wrinkles on her face, her step is slower, her hair is grayer. Years are bending her form. But she is beautiful still. Her nobility lies in the fact that being God's lady, she has expended herself unreservedly in fervent service to her family. And God has already begun to fashion her halo; soon He will crown her in the same beautiful gesture with which He crowned His own holy mother, Mary.

Milton Berle, whom millions of people love, once offered this tribute to his mother:

This is a tribute to someone whose memory I cherish and whose presence I miss. It is a tribute in song to my first love, my mother. To my friends who knew her she was warm, gay, a lady of carriage and dignity, but a forceful woman who gave her untiring devotion to the building of a career for her son. In my early years, Mother was my guiding hand. When I was outwardly daring, Mom was always there beside me. She was my eyes, my lips, my constant defender and companion. Mother gave up nights she could have spent in relaxation and days when she might have had enjoyment. She was my manager, my coach, my confidante. Mom's heart it was that held my fear when I was afraid; her head it was that became my pillow when I was weary.

She fought my battles the way few women could have done in this man's world of fight and show. The years went by, and as I grew older I learned to take care of my own problems, and Mother was there as my consultant, and she never gave up the job for which I needed her most—my closest friend.

Great men have always borne such witness to the good influence of mothers. Because her vocation comes from God, her qualities are from Him. These qualities carry a memory and a force that strongly influence every man at every moment of life. Who can tell what changes in the course of history are traceable to this quiet power. The Scriptures express her as possessing a sense of spiritual values—faith, courage, prayer, wisdom, joy, trustworthiness, dedication, kindness, and so forth. (Read, for example, Exodus 2:2–10; 1 Samuel 1:12–28; Proverbs 31:11, 26; and Psalm 113:9.) Scripture also points out her possessing active qualities— for example, keeping her house in good order, comforting, disciplining by putting up the STOP sign when needed. She is intent on living her life as a reflection of God's Word. (Read Psalm 78:4, 5; Proverbs 31:12, 27; Isaiah 66:13; Matthew 15:4; and Luke 2:19.)

As long as time will be, God will continue to bless men and women in the bond of love. As a man would be the head of a family, so a woman would be the heart. When their perfect love results in the birth of a child, husband and wife bloom into father and mother. Now there is a human trinity. What a glorious moment! God and man, God and woman, God, man, and woman becoming One in the creative act of giving human life!

How enriching it is to see every generation attempt to inspire mothers to become better mothers, and better mothers to become partners with God in giving and preserving human life. Motherhood is a challenging business. No matter how perplexing situations may be, there are always appropriate solutions to be found, if one would only stop, pray, seek Divine Guidance, and with Christian fortitude "look up," not "down." Nothing, nobody, should interfere with the Divine Rhythm and Program God purposely intends in His entrusting to parents the life of children.

I had the happy opportunity to visit with a mother right after she had given birth to her firstborn daughter. How beautiful she looked there in her hospital bed. Her own happiness and joy radiated from her whole person. Her every word reflected that inner felicity. She had experienced motherhood. And there nestled contentedly near her breast was her little infant. As we conversed, we shared the splendor of her special moment.

Then suddenly, raising her face to the ceiling, and then to me, she proclaimed: "Every child has a right to dedication. I owe it to this child. My child belongs to God first." When I heard those words I could not help but admire how a mother's beauty is *ministering* motherhood. Then with added sensitivity, she went on: "You know, Father, when you look at any infant you just have to say 'This is God's child. This child has come out of the Unseen. This child, my little bundle of joy, my little girl has been born into a redeemed world. Jesus died for her, too, you know.' "

This heightened my admiration even more. I cannot forget the sight of that mother and child. And as I contemplated one of God's greatest acts of creation, this young mother again spoke. This time very pensively. She did not smile. Her face became serious, if not almost sad. "This child is called by Divine Mercy to the inheritance of eternal life. This is God's supreme desire for this child, for every child! I wish every woman could feel the joy I feel at this moment. I wish every beautiful woman could experience that what we do with our children is a responsibility that only heaven and eternity can calculate."

Men will never be able to grasp the miracle of motherhood. It is too personal; it is too distinctive. Only the good Lord knows what possibilities are wrapped up in an infant cuddled in its mother's womb. What a tabernacle of grace, of life she is! Without God a parent is without chart or compass in seeing who and what both parent and child are, and where they are going. That moral responsibility will be rewarded with much blessing when such holy parents stand before the great throne of heaven at the final audit. One can almost hear Jesus say: "It is not a sin to be born—it is a sin to die without being born again. But come now, my faithful parents, come and receive the crown of your earthly splendor. Through your faithful parenthood, through suffering and sorrow, through joy and pain, through hardship and conquest, you have made the world come to recognize the dignity of a baby." Yes, "children are a heritage of the Lord: and the fruit of the womb is his reward." (Ps. 127:3)

I pray for mothers each day. In every mass that I am privileged to celebrate, in every holy hour I make for you, God's mothers are mentioned. Mothers, ask God to make you holy. Ask the Lord to make you worthy of your child's affection and trust. Jesus can inspire you. The mother and the child are like a fine gold chain: their bond is so close that nothing on earth can unlink them. No sin, no shame, no sickness, no horrible catastrophe, not even death, can separate them. Love binds them together. Their love transcends earth and ascends to the throne of God

Himself. This union of mother and child love is the reflection of God's own love.

A group of seminary students studying in Greece once came upon an ancient cemetery where they discovered some old weather-beaten headstones. They tried to brush away much of the earthly debris accumulated through the years. They read the lovely mottoes chiseled into the markers by the loved ones of those deceased. Then they came upon a special inscription. One of the seminarians translated the Greek words. The simple statement carved on the headstone was the best and the noblest tribute a child could ever render to a loving, self-sacrificing mother. It read simply: "She was a good mother."

I think the question as to whether or not one is a good mother can be resolved by asking this: As a mother blessed by God with life, are you willing to let God have His way? Are you willing to have God take absolute possession of your baby, your child? Will you allow our Lord to use that precious life for His glory in whatever manner He proposes without your ever objecting? If you do that, you are coming to the altar of God. Satan will hate you for that offering and dedication. He will even try to harass you, and even try to make you think that in later years your child is going astray, swerving from his Christian allegiance. But what you must do is to continue to renew your dedication. Like another St. Monica, you may have to wait it out, pray it out. But in the long run, God will crown your endurance with the sanctification of your child. Yes, it is possible to bind your sacrifice to the altar. Psalm 118:27 tells us: "Bind the sacrifice with cords, even unto the horns of the altar."

If you do this (and this may be the only act you can do), you will eventually experience a tremendous inner joy and fulfillment. Never give up prayer. Pray! Pray! Pray! It is the only spiritual strengthening you have. AFFIRM YOUR PARTNERSHIP WITH GOD! Be encouraged with Matthew 7:7 when he exhorts: "Ask, and it will be given to you."

Let us pray:

God, grant that my little child may instruct me in the way of you. Let his innocent eyes speak to me of the spotless holiness of Jesus. Let his open smile remind me of the great love you have for your creatures. Let his helplessness teach me your unbounded power. May his first feeble effort to speak call to my mind the wisdom of the Almighty. May my love for you be stimulated by the deep-rooted affection my child has for me. May I, in all these things, grow in appreciation of my precious holy motherhood.

And for us children, may this be our prayer:

I thank you, Lord Jesus Christ, for the love of my Mother which you have given to me. Of her was I born; through the years when I was helpless she cared for me. Her unselfish love has guided me. Remember her sacrifices, her devotions, her hopes. Lighten her burdens. Give her body and soul the joy of her love for you. You know, O Lord, the secrets of a mother's heart. Pray that my mother who with you and for you has treasured them as her own, may be united, here and hereafter, forever with you.

PART IV
The Value of
the Social Gospel

16.
The Gospel Message
of Healing

The healing of humanity is nothing else but the proclaiming of faith in the person of Jesus Christ. Evangelism begins with you and me. Our lives have been blessed by God in order to help another change his or her life. Your joy, my happiness, our zealous enthusiasm is to seek to give another a purpose. Our God is a God who seeks personal relationships. Our God is a God on the move! God is making Himself available to everyone. The Gospel proclaims love and concern for each other. You and I—EVERY HUMAN BEING from the moment of Adam's first breath to every breath that you and I take—are God's concern. God's love plan must influence you and me—EVERYONE—to subject ourselves to His will. Our thoughts, our speech, our interpersonal relationships should be the vehicle of preaching that God was in Jesus, sinless and spotless! Both you and I are called to teach, to preach, and to bring God's healing presence to a wounded humanity. May this chapter express God's invitation to you to share in His Divine Healing.

My own mission, as God has called me, is to preach and teach faith in the person of Jesus Christ. This is the Church's purpose, as Jesus Himself commissioned His first Apostles. (See Mark 16:15–20 and Acts 1:8.) While I am preaching about the Lord Jesus Christ, many souls are touched by the power of the Holy Spirit. They are enriched with Good News for a better and truer tomorrow. Through preaching en masse come signs and wonders en masse. These visible extraordinary manifestations of the Holy Spirit confirm the Gospel message. When that message is heard and accepted, we have the fruit of Christian evangelism: SALVATION!

During these sessions of preaching and teaching, I experience many avenues of healing insights while I am under what is known as the "Anointing of the Holy Spirit." At other times, by a gift known as the "Word of Knowledge," I am led by the Spirit to identify exactly the ailment or the person, or a combination of both. It is quite dramatic, extraordinary, intellectually baffling; yet it is convincing proof that GOD IS WORKING AMONG HIS PEOPLE. People experiencing these phenomena are so overwhelmed by the Spirit of God's Healing Love, that many come forth to give praise and thanksgiving and to witness to the assembled community.

But precisely what is the Gospel message of healing? What does God want you to know about HOLISTIC DIVINE HEALING?

● The revival of Christian Healing in the Church today may be a means of the greatest advance of Christianity in this century.

● It is a wonderful thing to know that when the Spirit prompts a person to speak to someone about Christ, He has been working in that heart and making it ready to receive that person's witness.

● Evangelism is nothing more than giving God's message of life in Christ —rendering it understandable to everyone and in every situation. As people become involved in the ministry of LISTENING, SERVING, and SPEAKING, they proclaim the thrill of their own religious experiences with the Lord.

● God's healing power operates within the Church, which is the Body of Christ on earth, through her membership.

● Anyone who loves the Church, God's people, with all his or her heart consciously suffers the spiritual crisis in the world.

● As healing was an important part of Christ's ministry, it is intended to be a part of His disciples' work in every generation. The Age of Miracles is not over!

● God invariably works through human channels to do His healing. We must make ourselves fit and willing channels.

● God uses many agencies for healing, some of which are prayer, medicine, surgery, psychiatry, psychology, the arts and sciences.

● God's desire for us is wholeness and health. The Salvation message is for the whole person: spirit, soul, and body.

● Christian Healing is accomplished through faith in Christ during the course of which the patient subjects his entire life to the scrutiny and counsel of God.

● Divine Healing states that God is the One who heals all of our diseases. (Ps. 103:3 and Acts 3:12–16) Miraculous healing consists in a striking INTERPOSITION of Divine Power by which the operations of the ordinary courses of nature are overruled, suspended, or modified. God has on occasions chosen to intervene in the cure of bodily ills in order to vindicate (justify, free, absolve) and increase human faith in His power. Many of Christ's miracles reflect this purpose. Even the Apostles and some of their successors in the infant Church were given this charismatic gift of healing for the same reason. These events are dependent entirely on the will of God beyond all human prediction. These Divine Interventions are continual throughout the centuries.

● The Christian message (the Gospel) of salvation presents sickness as connected with sin, not specifically personal sin (John 9:3–5). Still, sin flows from the Original Fall. Because of this, therefore, the question of a religious approach to its cure arises.

● In every age of mankind's history, Christians have sought recovery by means of skilled medical care (Ecclus. 38:1–15) and have always believed in the assistance of prayer and religious blessings. In other words, they believed in Christian Healing. Christians act properly and in accord with God when they pray for Divine Help—in illness or in any other tribulation. The cure of bodily sickness is included among God's blessings of salvation; and it is a special favor granted by God. God, Himself, says "For I, the Lord, am your healer." (Exod. 15:26) (NASB) Moreover, in Hosea 11:3, God says, "I took them in my arms; but they did not know that I healed them." (NASB) And so we see that to heal is to repair and to build up.

● Belief in Christian Healing does not preclude one from having recourse to medical care. Religion does not replace medicine. They both help in recovery. Medicine—God's natural gift of healing to us—offers direct action for the healing. It utilizes the biological, the chemical, and psychological realities. But the Christian Healing is a direct healing of the sick by Divine Power. It is an extraordinary intervention of God in the established order of nature and human life. It strengthens in grace the sick person and so is called "a miracle."

● In the New Testament, Christ's miraculous healing of the sick is one of the signs that the last messianic times have come. (Matt. 11:4, 5) Jesus conferred this power also to His Apostles; and they, in turn, also healed the sick. (Matt. 10:1) They did this by many means: preaching, teaching, casting out demons, laying on of hands, or anointing. (Mark 6:13, 15–18)

● According to Christian theology, FAITH or TRUST, CONFIDENCE or BELIEF, on the part of the sick is required as A CONDITION FOR THE CURE: IT IS NOT ITS CAUSE. (Matt. 13:58)

● Faith cures, or faith healing, is not to be confused with Divine Healing. Divine Healing offers a cure of an ailment, and it accomplishes such through religious faith. It depends on the mercy and love of God offered to us through the salvation message. On the other hand, a faith cure is healing by suggestion, psychological means, or through natural means such as medical treatment. It is not religious in character.

• Faith healing is the attempt to use Divine Power as if it were a natural and normal curative agent, blocked only by insufficient confidence on the part of the human sufferer. This is quantitative healing, dependent solely upon human conditions and natural factors working simultaneously. The phenomena claimed by faith healers are allegedly regular events, automatically evoked by sufficient human faith. This means that if the sick person is sufficiently persuaded that Divine Power can cure him or her, it will; or if the sufferer is not cured, it is because he or she has not had sufficient faith. THIS IS NOT DIVINE HEALING.

• A Christian must not subject himself or herself to faith healing practices that treat Divine Healing Power as the automatic servant of calculated human acts. Herein is a theological error implicit in the practice of faith healing; because by such, it is possible to scandalize others, or thrust a person into psychological or moral guilt, and perhaps harm one's health through neglect of normal medical treatment.

• Explanation for cures through such faith healing, which at times do produce healings, is usually PSYCHOSOMATIC rather than SUPERNATURAL. Such illnesses invariably are of a functional nature—such as hysterical paralysis, or certain kinds of asthma. They are not, however, organic diseases such as cancer, nervous and muscular disorders, lupus, and so forth. And, finally, faith healing accents that the mental attitude of the sufferer can play a great part in its increase or decrease. We find that hypnotists and psychotherapists treat such illnesses in essentially the same way the faith healer does.

• The faith healer attempts to implant in the mind "a suggestion" that will influence the body; and in the case of a religious person, this suggestion can have a potent effect. This is particularly true if within a healing ritual or ceremony there is activated a high pitch of mass excitement. Rousing, emotional oratory, in a highly charged atmosphere is able to break down the sick person's resistance to suggestion. What we need to preach in Divine Healing is the message of God's love, the episodes of Gospel stories, the compassion of Jesus toward sinners and toward the sick, the offering of God's love as our hope for redemption. In short, we must evangelize God's people by the Gospel message of total healing. And this is Jesus Christ, the Son of God, made flesh, our Divine Physician!

- There are no failures in Christian Healing. Exchanging one's problem for Christ induces peace and accelerates the healing processes.
- Jesus Christ lives today, and He still possesses *all power* on earth as in heaven.

17.

To Be Forgiven—
That Is the Great Healing

When a man becomes a new creature
in Christ, his old life has
disappeared, everything has become
new about him.

(2 COR. 5:17) (Knox)

To forgive another human person is healing. When God pardons the sinner, there is restoration. When Jesus cries out from the depths of His heart as He hangs there upon the Cross, "Father, forgive them, they do not know what they are doing," that is HEALING, REDEMPTIVE SALVATION! Everybody likes a new chance. Everyone needs a new opportunity to start all over again. You and I welcome those fresh new moments when we can write new chapters in the autobiography of our weak lives, lives so easily subjected to the wounds of a fallen human nature.

When someone has the grace to start all over again, his greatest consolation is that God through Jesus has "justified" his human frailty. Psalm 62:5–6 is very hopeful, as it is comforting: "Rest in God alone, my soul! He is the source of my hope; with him alone for my rock, my safety, my fortress, I can never fall."

As one rejoices over the chance for a new living, one is really perceiving that what St. Paul was mentioning in 2 Corinthians 5:17 is that when someone becomes a Christian, he or she is becoming a brand-new person inside. In other words, he or she is not the same anymore. A New Life has begun! But being human, we often meander in life, losing sight of the Divine Romance. Only when we are hurt through human encounters do we come to our senses and realize that God alone was He whom we were seeking.

God in His immense love for you, for all humankind, offers everyone the opportunity to experience the New Life. Those who accept God's offer find a quality of life that has meaning, purpose, power, and personal peace. Our heavenly Father calls it "Eternal Life." It is a life that *never ends!*

When one speaks of forgiveness, one is speaking of a soul, today's sinner who becomes tomorrow's saint. It doesn't take much time to become a saint; it only takes much love. That love, as small as it may be in its human expression, becomes a giant love response from Him, Jesus Christ, whom God sent to give us salvation as He forgives us through His healing benevolence.

The Way of the Lord is the Ministry of Healing. Healing is the product of Jesus' command to His twelve chosen missionaries. He fortified them with faith in Him first; then He directed them to the power of love through the expression of zeal. With zeal in their minds, with love in their hearts, they found themselves with an Apostolate—the Apostolate of Jesus' cause on earth—to go out and preach the Kingdom, to heal the sick. This is the full message of the Gospel. It is the salvation message. It touches individual personal lives, and it touches peoples and nations and every social issue that man can contrive.

The Way of the Lord is unique. It is a foundation truth. And being a foundation truth, it is good and it is applicable *to all times, to all circumstances, and to all conditions, to every man, woman, or child, to every creed and race. The Gospel Message of Healing/Salvation is for the world.*

The ministry of healing is not a separate activity within the Church, conducted by people with special gifts. It is the normal activity of God through Christ as it has been revealed to us in Jewish and Christian revelation. The Scriptures and the behavior of the Church throughout the centuries have always complied with this Christ-Healing-Salvific presence. It is wonderful to have a God not way "up there" and impersonal, but a good God *here* among us who really cares!

God is at work in the world with a purpose that existed before any person was called to share it. We can walk in the way of the Lord by living in such a way that God's righteousness, His justice and love, will be expressed not only in our individual lives and characters, but also in the social lives of all nations. The Church was founded to be only the instrument that the Lord would use for the fulfillment of His purpose for the world: to bring the Kingdom of God "on Earth as it is in heaven." This concept of the Kingdom of God is the very kernel of Christ's teaching so much so that without it the Gospel is stripped of its essential meaning.

The problem of evangelization today—as it was sometimes in the past

—is how to interpret the phrase "the Kingdom of God" into language that conveys the thrill of its meaning to a world that has lost all sense of purpose and hope for the future. There is a close connection between the Kingdom and the Healing Ministry of Our Lord. It is the obligation of the Church to go forth boldly in the name of Jesus and in the power of the Holy Spirit and to proclaim His presence, that He is the Messiah. It is the ministry of the Church to heal, that is, to restore God's spoiled and damaged creation unto wholeness, and to overcome evil and the effects of evil.

Jesus, the Master, was deeply conscious that His Father was at work in the world with the ultimate purpose of rebuilding broken humanity into wholeness. The Master's task would be to uplift you and me, and to point out the road to Divine Perfection. The Master said, as recorded in John 5:17: "My Father goes on working, and so do I." In John 10:29–30, Our Blessed Lord affirms: "The Father who gave them to me is greater than anyone, and no one can steal from the Father. The Father and I are one." Powerful indeed were the ministry signs of the Lord. "Get up, pick up your sleeping mat and walk. The man was cured at once, and he picked up his mat and walked away." (John 5:8–9) Tremendous is he who knows his authority. The Master knew who He was; He was conscious that the Father sent Him to build and not to tear down, to heal and not to hurt. "So the disciples asked one another, Has someone been bringing him food? But Jesus said: 'My food is to do the will of the one who sent me, and to complete his work.'" (John 4:34)

Did Jesus have a method? He had an authentic commission from heaven. He had to come: to be born of a sinless virgin conceived by the Holy Spirit, to do good, to preach and teach and heal, to suffer and be crucified, to be buried. He was to leave the tomb EMPTY! But what was the method—all the intermediary steps? We by our makeup are always looking for and depending on method. God forgive some of us! We at times look to methods for our renewed zeal and we forget the power of the presence of Jesus alive in us whom He called. If we would only let the Master have His way with us we would be fully alive! But what was Jesus' way? With Jesus there is only one way: the way of faith and trust in God. The way back to the Father as Jesus taught and healed was: REPENT! Matthew, who is definite in his presentation of the Kingdom, describes: "In those days John the Baptist appeared, preaching in the wilderness of Judea; 'Repent,' he said, 'the kingdom of heaven is at hand.' It was of Him that the prophet Isaiah spoke, when he said, 'There is a voice of one crying in the wilderness, Prepare the way of the Lord, straighten out His path.' " (Matt. 3:1–3) And he says it more precisely: "From that time onward, Jesus began to preach: 'Repent,' he said, 'the kingdom of heaven is at hand.' " (Matt. 4:17)

The second thing Jesus did was *to call his disciples.* He would take them alone into His presence, inspire them, influence them, empower them, strengthen them in faith, and then invigorating them with holy zeal tempered by prayer, He would send them out. How would He send them out? He would send them out in the power of the Holy Spirit. That is what Pentecost is all about. It is not the various gifts, which are only the means to extend the visible presence of the Lord (this is the nature of charisms and that is why charisms are so necessary for the Church); but the one Gift of Pentecost is POWER! And so, immediately they began to travel as "itinerant missionaries" into Galilee and its surrounding towns and villages, into Judea and its neighboring territories, along the seas and lakes, even into Samaria, with its pagan inhabitants. Slowly but visibly, God had come to speak, converse, communicate truth/Himself, blessing/His grace, healing/His salvation. And as they went they taught, and they preached the Kingdom, healing all manner of sickness. "And Jesus, with the power of the Spirit in him, returned to Galilee; and his reputation spread throughout the countryside. He taught in their synagogues and everyone praised him." (Luke 4:14–15) And again in Luke 6:17–19, "[These] had come to hear Him and to be cured of their diseases. People tormented by unclean spirits were also cured, and everyone in the crowd was trying to touch Him because power came out of Him that cured them all."

The Church is Christ personified; it is Christ continuing His purpose in every person from here to eternity. The Church without the Kingdom is an empty institution. The Church with the Kingdom is an organism of life: Christ is its head, invisible but real, dwelling powerfully in its visible successors "until the end of time." Yes, the Church and the Kingdom! The nature of the Church, then, derives its mission "to teach, to preach, to heal, to forgive" from the very nature of God. God's nature is that of community through which He proposes to perform His creative and re-demptive activity in the world. The Church exists *only* to interpret the Kingdom of God to the world. The Church, unless it is not divinely instituted, *can never forget* its commission. The Church will be until the end of time only that which the Lord intended it to be—nothing more! The Church is not an end in itself. It is the healing stream within all life.

It carries within itself the vision and the foretaste of God's Kingdom. It is the power of God! Confirming this belief, St. Paul preaches: (1 Cor. 12:12–13) "Just as a human body, though it is made up of many parts, is a single unit because all these parts, though many, make one body, so it is with Christ. In the one Spirit we were all baptized, Jews as well as Greeks, slaves as well as citizens, and one Spirit was given to us all to drink." Paul is probably referring to the rock that gave out water to the Israelites in the wilderness. It is not certain here to which sacraments he is alluding. But the general concept is clear that the Church brings this healing love to the people of God; and that life is Christ with all His power and might. This power of God challenges evil, and it overcomes it. And as it does, it gives NEW LIFE TO THE WORLD!

It ought to be clear then that the healing ministry of the Church is the ministry of Christ through His Body, the Church. God is at work among us today more than ever before. God is making Himself available to us. And the big question that we are asking now, by the unleashing of Divine Force, is "What is going on today with God?" The answer, again, is "God is a God on the move! And He is making Himself felt to everyone. He is demonstrating that He alone is adequate to our needs."

All throughout the two testaments, the one and only theme is that God is calling His people. All God ever wanted was a people restored, renewed, healed, *forgiven*, SAVED! This is seen in every ministry of healing. Lead my people to repentance; lead them to my heart. Lead my people into compunction; lead them to forgiveness. Let there be resurrected hope in my people; let it come alive through the living love of my son, Christ. Give New Birth to my people!

God is speaking to us dynamically, right now. And every time we hear the Shepherd's concerned voice, we can sparkle with new hope. When we hear His Divine Footsteps we become sensitized to His august presence. If everyone would only believe, there would be healing in every aspect of our being. The salvation message of Jesus and His Church is healing not only for the soul and spirit, but for the body as well.

In my crusades, often fifteen or twenty thousand people come at a time; they come from all over, from every walk of life. And they keep coming, coming, and coming. For both clergy and laity, it is a splendid dream come alive . . . to see so many wonderful people, so many loyal followers of God, so many leaders who are humble in their wisdom, so many different ethnic groups gather together as a people of God. They come because of their brokenness, but God has a plan of healing far superior than the condition of illness. They come with the tragedies of their humanity. They come as "pilgrims" traveling on their own journey. THEY COME LOOKING FOR HOPE! That is, in spite of life's perplexities, sorrows, and hardships, even though mingled at times with moments of pleasure and joy, they come to seek a rainbow, a more beautiful tomorrow.

We ask them, "Whom are you seeking?" As we purify their intentions, elevating their minds above their bodily needs and up to the Divine Physician, their voices ring out: "We come for some Good News!" Better still, "We come looking for the AUTHOR of that GOOD NEWS. WE COME FOR A SAVIOR." And even more profoundly, "We come looking for OUR LORD and MASTER. WE COME FOR JESUS CHRIST, SON OF GOD!"

Though in my crusades I serve these members of the Church, it is really they who are ministering to me. As I look around the vast arenas and stadia, I observe in the huge crowds many examples of mortal misery: broken lives, wounded spirits, deformed and decrepit bodies, decaying flesh and infectious diseases. There they are seated, standing, or lying on stretchers, jamming every doorway and aisle. People with babies in their arms, people with crutches, people in wheelchairs, people who are blind or deaf—the gamut of human tragedy united in the brokenness of sin and its consequences. Tragedy has a special way of bringing people together. United with them in the common bond of pain, we realize, we concretize, the gift of fellowship. There are no longer Catholics, Protestants, Jews, the churched or the unchurched. These distinctions are very insignificant when one is desperately in pain, perhaps even close to death. Humility has power to bring us to our knees.

In the bond of fellowship there are gathered only human beings looking up to the same God whose voice they believe Isaiah accurately reported: " 'Console my people, console them,' says your God." (Isa. 40:1) "Speak tenderly to Jerusalem and tell her that her sad days are gone. Her sins are pardoned, and the Lord will give her twice as many blessings as He gave her punishment before." Yes, in the bond of fellowship people find their journey of discovery; together they share friendship, love for one another. Their unity brings them into a greater oneness with God and all people. "These remained faithful to the teaching of the apostles, to the brotherhood, to the breaking of bread and to prayers. The many miracles and signs worked through the apostles made a deep impression on everyone." (Acts 2:42–43) Together they listen, they sing, they pray, they cry, they forgive, they love. They hear the message of Christ through the healing evangelist. Jesus is speaking to them. The Father calls them. The Lord leads them.

And when they experience the Healing Divine Physician they undergo a religious experience that GOD IS ALIVE. They leave different persons from what they were when they came. It is impossible not to. They have been *touched.* God has *forgiven* them.

18.
Responding to the Call
within Our Lives—Come Home

If I may borrow a thought from G. K. Chesterton, there are existing today *loud voices*—voices of anger, protest, and dissatisfaction, whether related to social, economic, or political conditions. Invariably, this is associated with a lack of honest introspection. One's lack of self-content-ment frequently prompts search for a "scapegoat." Could this be the cause of many defections in our contemporary Church? Have we consid-ered the Church in the foibles of its humanity as having jilted "those whom Christ called to arms"? Have we forgotten that the Holy Spirit is the infallible power of the Church's Pentecost? More basically still, has our manhood or womanhood been the real basis of our anger toward a Church that seems to be launching out into more general issues of con-temporary life? All issues that pertain to us and our history must include God. They are not necessarily less or more important than others, pro-vided they pertain to our recognition and affirmation that God does exist.

Our busy, contemporary age seems to advocate a need for time man-agement. Time management directs people to decide to allocate priorities about what is momentarily *urgent* or *important*. But, in defense of the absolute truth, that God is alive and that God is on the move, no leader —religious or civic—can overlook the importance and urgency of issues pertaining to God. These cannot be labeled as we label other "priorities." Be it the issue of prayer in schools or issues of human rights, the under-lining cause of God must be defended and protected. With the honor of God, there are no "lesser" or "more urgent" issues!

With loud voices, therefore, being raised in protest and in bitter criti-cism of religion and the Church, we might be fearing the worst. It may seem as though distrust and opposition are winning out over loving loy-alty to the faith. But the truth, Chesterton proclaimed, still holds valid today. As God's healing minister, I join my voice with his and I say to you "Let's not look down into the mud. Let's look up." Let us not be pessimistic in life; rather, with a Dale Carnegie approach and with trust in God's grace, we look at life in terms of what we can give and not take. I say to you: "COME HOME! COME HOME!"

Chesterton's words are timely because his words were based upon truth. Truth cannot be altered! Chesterton wrote in his *Autobiography:* "The moment men cease to pull against the Catholic Church, they feel a tug toward it. The moment they cease to shout it down, they begin to listen to it with pleasure. The moment they try to be fair to it, they begin to be fond of it. But when the affection has passed a certain point, it begins to take on the . . . grandeur of a great love affair."

A thoughtful observer of modern man's growing interest in God and religion has remarked that many men are turning to God today because "they never felt so helpless before. They always had some ace up their sleeve." But trump cards like progress or science or education—when divorced from God—turned out to be ghastly jokers, and the men who formerly wagered their souls for them are now thoroughly disillusioned.

The wonderful spread of the Church during the first three centuries of its existence is one of the proofs that it is a Divine Institution. That a religion preached in the little country of Palestine by one who was meek and humble of heart, and who chose a few humble fishermen to launch out into deeper waters with His message, to go into a world that was totally disheveled, and that in the space of three hundred years became mightier than pagan Rome, is truly the miracle-power of the Holy Spirit.

Our Blessed Lord said that His followers were to be called "Church," that is, *ecclesia.* This new *ecclesia* would start small. It would be something like a mustard seed, but it would grow into a great tree "so that the birds of the air would dwell under its shadow." (Mark 4:32) It would be a new society with other ideals. It would have new purposes and goals other than the world's. It would experience hate from a world that would hate Him and His way of life. His Church would be no narrower or broader than He Himself, the founder, Jesus Christ. His Church would in no way be able to alter His teaching any more than a judge could alter the Constitution or a decision of the United States Supreme Court. Truth could and can never be changed. Christ was the Truth and is the Truth. The Church which is His teaches what He taught, and that is why its doctrine is infallible. It is God's own. When many reject Christ, they are rejecting truth itself. When people leave the Church, they seem to do so in accord with their own views. By doing so, they reject His Church because it does not teach what they want to believe. But His Church, which He called, which He sent out, will always be crusaders for Christ.

Because of the sweat and tears of the Church, on the great day to come it is Christ's standard that will prevail—not the world's. And for this reason, therefore, the members of Jesus' Church would be so closely united to each other by being united in Him, that if anyone did any kind of act—good or evil—to any other member, he or she would be doing it to and for Him. To offer a person food, or a drink of cold water, would be to offer it to Him. If anyone persecuted another human being, tortured and imprisoned that human being, it would be done to Christ. This unity with Christ and the members of His Church is symbolized by Christ in the parable of the vine and its branches.

This new *ecclesia* or body of people was not to be like a club that is formed by persons coming together in a center for a common purpose. Rather, it was to be like a living body from whose center life would radiate. It would nourish the organisms of that mystical body. It would not consist of men and women who would make only a contribution to an "organization." The Church is not an organization. The Church is an organism. And for this reason, it would be Christ, the Head, who would fill each man and each woman, each human being with Divine Life. If there were a human analogy for this *ecclesia,* it would be the human body. A body is composed of millions of tiny cells, each one living its own individual life, and yet no one cell is able to live apart from the body. So this new *ecclesia,* or body, would be made up of millions of individuals who were incorporated into Christ. This is the *mystical body.*

The nucleus of this *ecclesia* or body was the Apostles who were destined to spread out over the whole world, to teach all nations even to the consummation of the world. They would go forth as leaders in this new *ecclesia* fortified, strengthened, armed with the weapons of Christ: truth and morality. Their witnessing message to the Resurrection of Christ which they had experienced would be their convincing tool. This belief that started with Christ and was given to His Church has endured for almost two thousand years among the most advanced nations of the world. It now professes itself throughout Christendom. It celebrates as a world holiday the birthday of its founder, Jesus Christ, and the birthday of its own existence with a worldwide festivity throughout all Christendom: Pentecost. And so to all men, women, and children, Christ speaks to "Come Home" to their roots because the Resurrection is and remains the greatest incentive and the greatest source of strength, peace, and joy.

Dr. Tom Dooley once stated: "Lose yourself in something greater than self." Mother Teresa, in a conversation with me in the Bronx, accented a similar theme: "Give your hands to help them and your heart to love them."

When God summons an individual to a determined service, He is actually orientating, gearing that person to community concern. What God is really doing is allowing that person to go out to share with another human being his or her own religious experience. As one witnesses to community, one brings also the miracle of affirmation—which is nothing more than a visible event that creates faith in another human being.

Such an affirmation is not used for egocentric or neurotic self-indulgence. It is not self-pity finding solace but it is an affirmation of authentic fulfillment. It is the giving and the living for another through a creative process of Divine Influence. It influences us and we, in turn, transmit this personal experience to another. In evangelical terms, this is called witnessing. This witnessing has as its analogy the light shining over darkness. It is the *lumen Christi*—the light of Christ.

Faith, in St. Paul's teaching, is precisely this experience. It commences with hearing God's word: "So faith comes from what is preached, and what is preached comes from the word of about Christ." (Rom. 10:17) When one with openness of heart and readiness of spirit accepts this Word, he or she responds to God's Divine Plan. As thus a commitment is made to the will of God, a person is saved with God's presence of peace. That person is justified through Christ alone who offers the saving power of the Almighty.

The challenging Call of Christ, His invitation, will always be one that urges our reception. If we are to be interiorly peaceful, affirmed and productive, we must receive His gift. "Follow me" Jesus says, and "I will make you into fishers of men. And at once they left their nets and followed Him." (Mark 1:17–18)

No one is forced to serve the Lord, though all are called. Each person is summoned to make a choice. This precise choice is to respond to the love of Him who is total love. A gift is not a gift unless you give it away. God gives His love away to us: "Yes, God loved the world so much that He gave His only Son." (John 3:16) In accepting the gift to serve, we become Christ's personification to the world.

The response may cost us something. Everything worthwhile does. The cost of answering God's call is unconditional surrender to the immediate needs of God's people. When we answer God's call, he bestows the power of Pentecost on us—the power to serve.

What do we share with community by our own personal response of love to God? We offer our brokenness; but the brokenness we share with others is one that God had taken, purified, and resurrected. Through God's magnificent mercy, our own brokenness becomes beautiful. It becomes an example of resurrection to another soul who is in search. As we allow this, we recognize the supreme responsibility and mission task of the universal Church. We are thus committed to the work that Christ has mapped out for all who would follow in His footsteps.

What is the supreme task of the Church? Some may be surprised to know that the supreme task of the Church is not renewal. It is to preach the Gospel of Jesus Christ to every creature, whether the skin color is black or yellow, red or white. The one job of the Church is to reach the whole world, the entire humanity, with the Gospel. "You will receive power when the Holy Spirit comes on you, and then you will be my witnesses . . . to the ends of the earth." (Acts 1:8)

What are we called to serve? We are called to serve the BODY OF THE CHURCH because each person is a member of the whole body of Christ. Those who serve do so as healthy cells replenishing infected cells or cells in need of nourishment—thus putting the broken Body of Christ together.

God never calls a man or a woman to service without equipping him or her for that service. Perhaps at times, for reasons that are very sensitive and personal, the one who is called may find that he or she resists the Lord, at least at the beginning. We may also find ourselves at war—the battle between self-aggrandizement and the causes of the Almighty that summon us on. But then, are not uncharted waters quite frightening? Are we not fearful of a darkened forest? On the other hand, does not a peace settle upon us as we remember the joy and the thrill that were ours when God whispered: "Son, daughter, my child, my friend, I'll take what you have and I will use it."

To serve the Church at large faithfully necessarily involves service to the local church. Every local church must become more clearly aware of its particular position in the ministry of the universal Church. For it is in this light of faith that the local church draws its strength to live, strive, and grow. Some believers may need to expand their knowledge in this regard. The local church needs to delve deeper into the nature of vocation and mission of the people of God. It must journey with the people of God toward its eternal homeland.

God's people thrive on the power of obedience to legitimate authority. A hierarchy must exist not for the purpose of lording over subjects, as a head over a body. It gives wisdom flowing from understanding, it offers faith and promotes zeal. There must, therefore, be a clear understanding of the identity and role of the bishop, the priest, the deacon, and the religious—most especially their irreplaceable missions and their service to the people of God.

There is much conversation and discussion about renewal in the Church. There is likewise much emphasis on those in Holy Orders, vis-à-vis those in the ranks of the laity. The objective truth, however, remains unalterable: those in Holy Orders are the authentic commissioned leaders. Regardless of personal likes or dislikes, the truth remains that the Lord has called these servants to lead us to eternity. Each generation has its own determined time. Valid renewal can be accomplished only in the heart of the Church through the priesthood. To fulfill this goal, the priesthood itself must experience internal renewal in that power that always belonged to it by consecration: the Holy Spirit. "This is why I am reminding you now to fan into a flame the gift that God gave you when I laid my hands on you. God's gift was not a spirit of timidity, but the Spirit of power and love and self-control. So you are never to be ashamed of witnessing to the Lord or ashamed of me for being his prisoner; but with me bear the hardships for the sake of the Good News, relying on the power of God." (2 Tim. 1:6–8) And this is the precise power that Archbishop Fulton J. Sheen, when he was a monsignor, used to speak to us about: the power of the Holy Spirit to influence. He used to say to us: "If there is ever any gift that you should ask God for, let it be the power of the Holy Spirit to influence others unto holy commitment."

The whole Church, both Catholic and Protestant, needs in this our modern day a fresh Baptism of the Holy Spirit. Pentecost is not a denomination; it refers to the feast day when the Apostles were first filled with the Holy Spirit. This infilling of the Holy Spirit is an endowment of power for every Christian, whether Catholic or Protestant, as well as for potential Christians. Pentecost has a purpose. That purpose is startling and impelling. Its message unveils a power which multitudes have bypassed. Jesus said: "You will receive power." Power for what? What do we believe we should accomplish with this power?

It is the power to bring about evangelization; and evangelization will be confirmed by signs and wonders and many miracles. When the Holy Spirit comes into us with His presence of distinctive power, we become channels for evangelization. We share with another our own religious experience of prayer with God for our conversion. Whether one is comfortable in calling this experience the Baptism of the Holy Spirit or an actual grace of God is really unimportant. What is important is that the Lord caresses the world—and He does so through men and women. What a tremendous grace it is to be called, to be chosen, to be life for one another!

What is your particular call? What is your response as you observe God's world? If you have really accepted Him wholeheartedly, if you intend to serve Him unconditionally, your response can only be: *adsum,* "here I am, Lord."

19.
The Great Physician

Dear God, I look about and I see the anguish and the pain of man. The depths of my soul cry out "What can I do?" Dear God, my humanity craves to heal. But why have you moved my heart so? For some reason, unknown to me, you have chosen me from so many more capable than I to be a physician. Yes, I am bound to the dictates of medicine. I am an instrument of healing. Oh, how I tremble as I ponder this awesome responsibility! It is your work, oh Lord, not mine. Without you I know I cannot succeed. Lord, you have placed in my human hands the bodies of the sick. Give me your skill. Help me to have clear vision—your vision! Fill my heart with authentic sympathy, kindness. Do help me to overcome every temporal weakness. Strengthen me with whatever may enable me to protect and preserve life. Lord, human life is precious to you. You have consigned it to the earth as a gift of your infinite love; you have eternalized it. Lord, you are the Great Physician. Before you I humbly bow in adoration. Before you I plead the cause of my vocation. Lord, make me worthy!

I consider this a wonderful opportunity to offer tribute to the great "giants of the medical profession." Above all, it is my distinctive joy, as a priest of God, blessed with the charismatic anointing of healing, to honor these men and women who distinguish themselves in one of the most noble professions in the world.

In the name of wounded humanity, I raise my voice in humble gratitude and honor to all those colleagues in the medical profession who jointly associate and assist in the various marvelous phases of this most remarkable corporal and mental work of mercy. As one standing before God and man, as intercessor/priest, I beseech the Almighty God to embellish and bestow upon each of these messengers of healing the choicest blessings of the Divine Physician. May the Almighty Creator, Provider, assist these medical servants; may He constantly walk with them, inspire them, guide them. May He be their reward as they experience the joys and the privilege of sharing God's healing spirit to a wounded and ailing humanity. In moments of sensitive trial, may God alone be their dauntless strength. In this modern day, indeed, the trials and the perplexities pertaining to modern science and technique cause many moments of anguish. Indeed, these trials, these perplexities, are not only many; they are tremendously serious.

Have you ever stopped to consider that these men and women, dedicated to medicine and life science are in actuality "apostles" of the Divine Physician? As in the mind of God, so in the minds of these medical experts, human life is precious because it is the gift of a God whose love is infinite; and when God gives life, it is forever. Did you not know that the undercurrent theme of joy in a man or woman of medicine ensues from the everlasting principle of RESPECT FOR LIFE? These ambassadors of compassion and healing walk out into the arena of illness to embrace with hands of flesh and hearts of determination, to eradicate diseases of all sorts. Some of these great giants of medicine not only caress human flesh at its worse, but, at times, must delve deeper. How often a physician's eyes perceive that the biggest disease today is not just leprosy or tuberculosis, but rather the feeling of being unwanted, uncared for, and deserted by everybody.

Pain is indicative of wounds. At times one must amputate; at other moments one must medicate; but in both instances he or she who is called to heal utilizes an acute mind, more telling than an X-ray machine. Bewildering as it may seem, a healer necessarily experiences helplessness. So very often all that he or she is able to do is offer some material cure for physical pain, when what may be needed is remedy for inner anguish.

Wounds are many! Hurts are so deep! Pain and suffering are evil, and ache often stems from the wound of lack of love and charity. So often the aching soul experiences terrible indifference toward both himself and his neighbor. There is nothing so disturbing as one who must continue to live as a stranger by the roadside—assaulted by exploitation, corruption, poverty, and disease.

Is there anyone to tend these wounds? After all, they are *real!* Beneath them are men and women. They have flesh and blood; they have immortal souls! To whom, indeed, can afflicted men and women, overwrought by sickness and diseases of all sorts, turn? God has a remedy. He is the primary healer through the Divine Healing Spirit. His secondary healer, who eradicates sickness and disease from the face of the earth, is well proclaimed in Scripture:

Honor the doctor with the honor that is his due
In return for his services;
For he too has been created by the Lord.
Healing itself comes from the Most High,
Like a gift from a king.
The doctor's learning keeps his head high,
He is regarded with awe by potentates.
The Lord has brought medicines into existence from the earth,
and a sensible man will not despise them.

Ecclus. 38:1-4

Do you realize that it is over two millennia since Christ placed His footprints in the sands of this earth? He left indelible memories. They are even more deeply engraved than those cut within the "rocks of ages." Then, as now, He still walks our lands. Then as now He continues to unfold the only story He ever proclaimed. He spoke and taught about the "Kingdom of God" as being fulfilled through His person. When people think of Him, they almost always immediately recall the many recordings of His magnificent power over the elements of the universe. They cannot help but remember His genuine and sincere compassion. They remember Him healing. He was and is the Divine Physician.

Times may change, but attitudes, disposition, traits never do. As Jesus has never changed, so neither does human nature. People all over the world are still suffering the wounds and the effects of original sin. Its consequences, as we know, are sickness, disease, death. Every man, woman, and child, therefore, has always looked for a healer of wounds. Today, as in times past, people are interested in being served. They desperately want the very best of life, activity, security, perennial satisfaction. And this is just as true of those in the Kingdom of God. Yet a servant attitude is one of the most important characteristics of godly men and women, of those who follow Jesus Christ.

The Apostles, Luke and Paul, made it very clear that they were gifted evangelists and teachers. But they made it clearer that a servant attitude was the only key to authentic ministry. Paul himself in his second letter to the Corinthians states forcefully: "It is not ourselves that we are preaching, but Christ Jesus as the Lord, and ourselves as your servants for Jesus' sake." (2 Cor. 4:5)

Other men and women of God have likewise adopted this attitude—servants of God and of other humans. As God was repeatedly referring to Moses, the great leader of Israel, as "My servant," so is He repeatedly overjoyed to identify the leaders of *His People* as "My Servants." Men and women of the medical profession are such servants; they are apostles of the Lord, the Divine Healing Physician. How great and memorable is that medical man or woman who allows Jesus, the Son of God, to be the inner Spirit of Healing, to use a man or a woman's hands, mind, skill to alleviate someone's wounds. How noble indeed is such a vocation!

As servants they personify the characteristics of servanthood. In humble service they clearly reveal what a servant ought to be. They do nothing out of selfish ambition or vain conceit. Who does not like going to a professional person who prizes the interests of others above his or her own? Patients can readily perceive this. They see and they know who serves with a concern that is *real,* the professionals who serve for what they can give and not for what they can get out of it. That patient who, when walking into a doctor's office is sincerely esteemed as worthy to be served, is already half-healed. Somehow these patients know that in that office, in the hands of that doctor, they are viewed not as a "thing," not as an interruption or burden, not as a "case," but as an opportunity to share Jesus' privilege to serve another human being.

20.
The Art of Conscious Healing

Every person naturally seeks affirmation. In acquiring it, one establishes oneself in a distinctive place. That person can change the world. Hearing the voice of destiny, each man, each woman, must go! They must answer that summons! Each of us wants life. We were made for life—not just a spark of it—but the whole *flame!* We do not seek death; death will eventually find us. And so, it is up to us to choose in life the road that makes death a fulfillment! Such is the mark of giants.

Among the great giants, as we mentioned in the last chapter, are the giants of medicine. They have been among us from the very beginning of time. Assuredly, one of these great giants of medicine was Hippocrates. Called the Father of Medicine, he lived in the third and fourth centuries before the birth of Christ and was one of the first to advance new approaches in the healing art. The history of medical achievement has always been a story with many turning points. Such advance often frightens the novices, the apathetic, those who are timid to launch out into deeper waters to discover the infinite greatness of God's creations. Life is filled with new approaches, with new and different possibilities and directions. A student of music cannot go through life only in the key of C. There are many more exciting scales to learn; and when they are mastered, the joy in this new discovery is exhilarating.

This wonderful father of medicine, Hippocrates, built both on those giant moments of progress that came suddenly and those that took years of painstaking research, as well as others that sprang forth because of entirely new concepts in thinking.

Such achievements were really great leaps for medical science. More than specific, spontaneous discoveries, they were made from ideas. An idea then becomes a method, a philosophy. And so, we are indebted and grateful to Hippocrates for his revolutionary approach. It has positively influenced the field of medicine from its primitive, pagan, and savage concepts, in the ages when people really believed that sick men and women were inhabited by a devil or other evil spirits. It has been pointed out that people of those times thought that the demons of darkness were displeased; that they invaded a person in order to inflict punishment. The primitive doctors knew nothing about bacterial infections. They had no idea whatsoever about the automatic spread of microscopic organisms conveying diseases. Their erroneous religious concepts purported a conscious and malignant siege on a person because the supernatural evil force was "displeased."

Of course, this is far from the Christian theology about sickness and disease. The Christian faith purified the Old Testament biblical concept about suffering. To be completely grasped, the Christian theology concerning Divine Healing merits a few reflections at this point. If the true value of the Christian or ethically upright doctor is to be recognized, then suffering from the biblical concept necessarily must be understood.

Exactly what is the biblical concept concerning suffering? The Old Testament, needing its purification in the coming of Jesus Christ, the proven messenger and prophet of the Almighty Father, definitely believed that suffering is a manifestation of human mortality. Suffering, for the pre-Christian intellect, was definitely an evil that should not have existed in a world supposedly created *completely good.* The pre-Christian mind based its reasoning upon the scripture of Genesis 1, the story of creation—that God made all, everything, good!

In pagan thought, then, every evil, every disease, and every sort of suffering was seen to derive from the *Kingdom of Death* in order *to menace men.* The death of an individual is the final act of suffering. And it is the ultimate conquest of death over the lives of men and women.

What an awful trauma this type of thinking caused! And today some people still think in a similar fashion. This sort of thinking was and is very crushing; it necessarily demanded an explanation—better still, an answer. The answer was attempted repeatedly throughout the Old Testament. But, as wanderers without a compass, people kept finding the proffered answer to be inadequate. Finally, with the coming of Christ, the essential significance was explained. Through the revelation of Christ's life, passion, death, and Resurrection, suffering took on a different focus: it was identified as a means of Divine Transformation for men. The anguishing Theory of Retribution was rectified through the alchemy of Christ-Among-Us. Christ purified the Theory of Retribution, which held and taught that suffering and death are the inevitable lot of man; that it flows from the sin of Adam and Eve, who ruptured the Divine Order of God's creation by their act of deliberate disobedience—their pride, their inner formal sin; that suffering then enters the world as a direct punishment of sin; and that forever after, sin and suffering are intimately connected. (Gen. 3:16–24)

The Theory of Retribution also falsely promulgated that very often God Himself directly or indirectly, when He would work through agents, was identified as *the cause* of suffering because He Himself is the cause of every created existing thing. And so, this was the manner in which the problem of suffering, disease, sickness, and death were explained by the Old Testament. God, according to this solution, is falsely perceived as a punitive Deity. He punishes actual sin with suffering; and the sinner can expect only sorrow and pain, whereas the just person can look forward to health and prosperity.

The Christian rejoices with just the opposite theory. For the Christian there is DIVINE HEALING! God is the one who heals all diseases. (Ps. 103:3 and Acts 3:12–16) This is the extraordinary way. It is supernatural in action. And as God does this, the ordinary laws of nature are not destroyed; they still exist. But God, for special purposes of His own, supersedes His own lesser laws. These events are dependent entirely on the will of God. They are beyond all human prediction. And throughout the centuries of life, these Divine Interventions have been witnessed. God had—and has—a solution for sickness, pain, death: He sent His only Son. His Son taught, preached, offered salvation for the *whole* person.

It is the task of Christian theology to investigate the manner in which religious healing is applied and factualized. The teachings of theology must always seek the salvation of a soul. That must be the final ultimate goal, namely, union with God.

God brings His healing to mankind in many ways, but two are essential here: miracles and anointing.

1. The Theology of Miracles

This is the most potent of Divine Healings. It is the miraculous way. As already noted in Chapter 16, it is nothing else but the absolute intervention of God. Though God's natural laws are still in existence, God for this particular moment, suspends his natural laws and intervenes directly to produce a Divine Love Expression upon a natural situation. The explanation is nothing else other than the fact that nothing natural is able of itself to restore health. All medical care proves helpless.

It should be especially noted that church authorities investigate meticulously such claimed "miraculous" healings. It must prove that there was a supernatural Divine Intervention over the laws of nature.

2. The Sacrament of Anointing

From the Cross of Christ every Christian can derive God's graces of the full atonement. Through the sacrament of the anointing, health is restored. It involves prayer and the application of Holy Oil. This is not miraculous healing per se. It is a sacramental healing. What happens is that the sacramental grace of anointing increases sanctifying faith, trust, love, and the gifts that go with the grace given as a spiritual remedy against sickness. Countless healings through the history of its use are proof that this sacrament is truly apt to act favorably on the body as well as on the soul and spiritual needs. Ontologically it enriches the person. It manifests itself even psychologically as it increases trust, courage, and holy fortitude. One beautiful effect is that it strengthens the whole person, the body not excluded. And this helps toward recovery. As a religious character it produces union with God. Christ is experienced in Christian theological faith. Christ is seen as Divine Healer.

Christians act properly when they pray for Divine Healing. They are acting in accord with their Father in Heaven when they seek His help during times of illness. They do this in times of any tribulation. The cure of bodily sickness is among God's blessings of salvation. It is a special favor granted by God.

In the New Testament our Blessed Lord utilized miracles to accent positively HIS DIVINE MISSION. He did not use miracles to prove who He was. He came to preach the Kingdom. He said that the Kingdom was at hand with His presence alive. And so, for this reason, His miraculous healings of the sick is one of the signs that the last messianic times have come. (Matt. 11:3–5) Likewise, as we saw elsewhere, the Apostles also received this power. As they preached the incredible truth of the Resurrection, the signs and wonders had to abound. All that was requested for Divine Healing was faith in Jesus.

It must be stressed again, however, that belief in Christian Healing does not preclude a sick person from having recourse to medical care. God usually works through His created natural channels. We are all sacraments of His grace. If we place ourselves in the hands of God, we each can become God's hands, God's heart, God's feet, God's love and concern. We can become Christ to one another.

God inspired men and women to survey, investigate, disclose the secrets of this vast universe. The answers to our problems lie within our very creation, if we would but just search for them. Among these, of course, are religious factors. They help recovery not as medicine does by acting directly on the level of biological, chemical, or physiological realities. The point of importance is that Christian Healing strengthens the grace life of the sick person; and sometimes it does this by the full force of an authentic miracle. No natural cause can explain it. The healing stands up to any scientific investigation. Isn't God a good God! All we have to do is give Him that chance to love us with His full presence.

For thousands of years, the art of medicine has been a very personal experience. It has been a relationship between a person who needs healing and the person who offers healing to him. Technology has added a new facet to a doctor/patient relationship: the machine. And ever since that third party came into the relationship, people have feared the impersonality it represents. In some ways, healing seemed a procedure, a dehumanizing experience. Doctors who serve the sick, conscious that the patients before them are human beings, will be contented giants of medicine only when they have not allowed machines to come between them and their patients. A doctor derives satisfaction from objective medical care that includes taking time to make that care personal. Human beings need to feel human, not humiliated. Only the personal touch of sincere compassion can break the barrier of grief.

Some patients have flesh wounds or burns. Others can't walk. Some ache with back problems or neuromuscular damage. Others have suffered strokes. They look at their wounds, wounds of all sorts. Dispiritedly they may say, "How ugly!" They are gripped by apathy and depression. But the giant doctors and nurses know how to offer positive strength. When patients have such personal interest shown, they respond much better to therapy. They make great progress. Above all, they learn to accept themselves.

Our bodies, minds, and souls will always search for the art of conscious healing. This art of conscious healing began with man himself. He sought to heal himself from his own human natural resources. If we observe the animal kingdom, we also see that the animal itself practices natural healing. Haven't you ever watched your dog or cat, or any other animal, lick its wounds? At other times the animal rolls over in the grass, in the dirt, in the mud. The animal does this because these are natural means of healing. The only trouble with this is that these are not systematic methods. The sentient animal performs these acts blindly, unconsciously, to relieve itself from physical pain.

With humans, on the other hand, attempts were made to immediately control suffering. Using conscious thought instead of instinct, man protected himself with appropriate clothing, adequate shelter. As we do to-day, so did early mankind attempt to fight diseases. Many of the illnesses we experience today were prevalent undoubtedly in prehistoric times. The common cold has always been with us, and certainly not as a friend. Arthritis, heart diseases, were not strangers. Unlike the animal, humans resorted to their intelligence systems for healing. And by word of mouth they passed this knowledge on to their descendants.

Interestingly enough, it was at the point of man's early experience with sickness and healing that superstition entered. The elders or tribal chief-tains, for reasons of their own, began to interpret through their witch doctors or shamans that abusers or lawbreakers were being punished by evil entities entering within. (Many of us have seen movies portraying witch doctors dressed in frightening costumes.) They would perform some cannibalistic ritual; shaking their rattles frantically, they attempted to arouse and dispel the disease. It was like a "counter-magic." Do you remember some of our grandparents' old remedies—brewed potions and herbs? Sometimes they worked. But all these practices only served to combat war, so to speak, against the unknown world of disease.

With the unfolding of his life on earth, man matured. By trial and error, success and failure, he began to progress in scientific method. Soon he practiced some crude surgery. He attempted to release fluids from the head or from other parts of his body. But these were very crude arts of healing; and for thousands of years ignorance prevailed. Nevertheless, it was a beginning. Regardless of methods, the one common concern was to relieve another human person from pain, suffering, and disease.

Today, step-by-step, the art of medicine proceeds victoriously well. Through exacting research, exhausting experimentation and testing, the human mind, spirit, and body are being better understood. Mystery still pervades many areas of human existence. But superstition has been com-bated in most civilized lands. In today's age we experience the outgrowth of the Golden Age of Medicine as it scientifically began over three centu-ries before Christ in Greece. Ethical human philosophies now rule; ethics of medicine have developed. And the doctors of each age have emerged as professional giants of medicine in their own right. We honor these professionals of healing.

Perhaps for this reason, the good God above allowed the illustrious giant of medicine, Hippocrates, to compose the doctors' medical code of ethics. It reflects the most humanitarian sensitivities that should exist between a patient and a doctor. For surely, a patient is more important than a disease. This oath has made and continues to make—for those doctors who still desire to be honorable—respected men and women, trustworthy enough to care for the life of a human being. It remains one of the most important documents of medical history:

THE HIPPOCRATIC OATH

I will look upon him who shall have taught me this Art even as one of my parents. I will share my substance with him, and I will supply his necessities, if he be in need. I will regard his offspring even as my own brethren, and I will teach them this Art, if they would learn it, without fee or covenant. I will impart this Art by precept, by lecture and by every mode of teaching, not only to my own sons but to the sons of him who has taught me, and to disciples bound by covenant and oath, according to the Law of Medicine.

The regimen I adopt shall be for the benefit of my patients according to my ability and judgment, and not for their hurt or for any wrong. I will give no deadly drug to any, though it be asked of me, nor will I counsel such, and especially I will not aid a woman to procure abortion. Whatsoever house I enter, there will I go for the benefit of the sick, refraining from all wrongdoing or corruption, and especially from any act of seduction, of male or female, of bond or free. Whatsoever things I see or hear concerning the life of men, in my attendance on the sick or even apart therefrom, which ought not to be noised abroad, I will keep silence thereon, counting such things to be as sacred secrets.

PART V
The Value of the
Resurrected Christ

21.

Victory with Honor

It is Easter Sunday. The month is April; the day is the twenty-second. The year is 1984. I have spent this week by God's special privilege in spiritual retreat. Hidden away in the requiem of silent prayer and meditation, appreciating the surroundings of the Mohawk Valley in New York State, which encircles the North American Jesuit Martyrs' Shrine. I personally have prayed for you. During this grace-filled Holy Week, I have prayed for all the people with whom the good Lord has allowed me to live, work, and spend my mortal existence. You are precious to God. And with Paul to the Philippians, I too proclaim the joy within me to give thanks to my God for all my memories of you, happy at all times in my prayer I offer for all of you. To share in the Church's privilege to bless you in the name of the Lord is truly both an honor and a responsibility.

In the foregoing reflections we did not stop at our human weaknesses; but we have looked beyond the quagmire. In looking up to God, our creator and our ultimate end, we have accentuated our human strengths. Placing them in the alchemy of God's love, we obtain new vision for a better tomorrow. "Where there is no vision," Solomon said, "the people perish." It is lamentable to see the enormous number of people who perish each year in the battle for self-emergence, affirmation, and self-survival. It is lamentable because these wonderful people could have lifted themselves to see a rainbow of hope. They could have done this if they had only looked up to their true constant source, namely, their God. With just a little more loyalty, just a little more waiting it out, a little more healthy and properly directed ambition, a little more enthusiasm, each one of them would have inevitably become a VICTOR. Each would have experienced a new chapter in his or her autobiography. With God's ever-faithful grace, each one of them would have had a religious experience in faith. God would have graced them with a New Birth!

This new experience of God ALIVE in us means new insights, new convictions, new rededication. We experience the power of the Resurrected Christ. It is this Christ who baptizes us afresh in the Baptism of the Holy Spirit. And all the potential good lingering within our beings suddenly bursts through our tombs. We are no longer deadwood, apparently good for nothing. We COME ALIVE! No longer do we need to wander in search of the great Albatross. But we go forth to witness the power of God living within each of us. Our tombs are empty! And in this newborn religious experience, we daily drink from the Holy Grail. Through our wanderings we have found our God.

God in His infinite constant love for you and me is always using things —big things, small things—to make something dramatic happen to us. He has a way of sending something that stops us in our tracks. It makes us think seriously about everything from a different perspective. If we allow Him to have His way, we perhaps can allow Him to change the very course on which we are meandering. Splendid as this New Chance/ New Birth may seem, there still remains the objective condition that you and I are responsible with our free will. We have to do more than just *think* about it. We must *do* something *with* it. When you and I do something about it, we can see that new vision. We really get our thinking straight! We have unraveled the spirit of the quest.

Like Bunyan's hero, Christian, you too must reflect:

As I went through the wild waste of this world, I came to a place where there was a den, and I lay down in it to sleep. While I slept, I had a dream, and Lo! I saw a man whose clothes were in rags, and he stood with his face from his own house, with a book in his hand, and a great load on his back. I saw him read from the leaves of a book, and as he read, he wept and shook with fear. Then he let out a loud cry, and said, "What shall I do to save my soul?"

Pilgrim's Progress

The thoughts expressed within the previous chapters will be in vain if they do not produce revival in you. If you have purchased this book, you certainly then are seeking inspiration. You do want a revival in your person, a new chance in life. Who doesn't? Who is the person who does not appreciate a new start? Everybody who has erred longs ardently for a RESURRECTION!

Don't you personally want this "quickening" restoration? Of course you do! The word "quicken" implies not only resurrection of a dead body, but a renewal of strength and vitality of the whole living person. When you individually experience revival you are acquiring a moral sensibility, a religious realization of "life again." For revival means the renewal of something that was once active and alive in you but that has since become dead or dormant.

If your religious experience in faith is authentic sound revival, you are undergoing the joy of the Church. Revival brings the Church back to its first love of Jesus who is not dead, but risen! When the Church begins to walk in the power of the risen Christ Jesus, its message is irresistible to the sinner, to the wanderer, to the one in need of a Rainbow of Hope. When this happens, society will have its answers to truth and morality. Society will turn to godliness, and God will heal the land! (2 Chron. 7:14)

If you want to benefit from this reading, you will have to make a journey to the Tomb of Jesus. But, like the women and the Apostles who went there in their human poverty, in their humble brokenness, in their perplexities and confusion, you need not stay at the TOMB! Be bold.

Go *into* the tomb! Look! What is it you see? THE TOMB IS EMPTY! HE HAS RISEN, as He said. God is ALIVE! He is NOT DEAD! All you need do now is build your new life upon that truth, upon THAT witness.

When Our Lord was training the twelve men whom He had chosen to continue His work of salvation, His first care and main preoccupation was to implant and develop FAITH in their souls, FAITH in the Divinity of His person and of His mission, in the divinity and truth of His religion. He so often said to them: "Trust in God still, and trust in me." (John 14:1) He kept insisting on Faith in Him. It seemed that He was telling them: "Listen, men! Tomorrow I am going to be sent to the Cross. You will look at me and you will doubt me. But have faith. Believe in me! I will keep my word. TRUST me!"

The Master kept telling the Apostles, kept extolling before them the power of faith. Faith alone can subdue the demons, make serpents and poisonous drinks harmless, cure diseases, and even move mountains. Jesus kept emphasizing the absolute necessity of faith for eternal salvation: "He who believes and is baptized will be saved." (Mark 16:16) He made them the witnesses of His miracles in order to confirm and increase their faith; He praised before them the faith of the centurion and of the Canaanite woman; and on several occasions He even rebuked the Apostles for their lack of faith.

After the Last Supper, Jesus prayed very intently that the FAITH of Peter, who was to strengthen his brethren in their belief, might not fail. (Luke 22:31–32)

If you have experienced joy from this book, then I feel sure that you are ready to live afresh again. That you are going to live in a spirit of trust and surrender. You WILL believe in the paschal nature of daily living. You will hope in His promise for eternal life. Then and only then can you relate to other people as brothers and sisters who have a common FATHER!

This new birth is a soul-winning experience! It is an inner miracle. This inner miracle is founded upon simple faith. Having experienced this yourself, you then can go forth and help others experience the miracle of the New Birth. God is using you then to bring forth the Social Gospel by redeeming society and culture with your witness to the Resurrected Jesus. Because of your rich revival experience, other people who are probably walking in a darkened forest will in turn accept the Risen Lord. They will see Him as the LIFE of the NEW BIRTH which SAVES them from evil, from sin, from sickness, from disease, and ultimately from death and hell. Eternal life will be theirs!

Would you receive the Lord right now, right from where you are. You may never have this chance again. God's grace wants to touch you right now, just where you are. O, why must God love us so much! But He does. He loves YOU! Yes, YOU, just as you are. Accept right now this opportunity for being born again, for revival, for renewal. The theology for being "born again" is there for all religious denominations. The only difference is not in the truth about salvation, but in the way salvation is received. It is in the process of Christian initiation that we see the difference. This simply means the process by which a particular denomination or church group initiates/accepts new members of that particular assembly. But these apparent differences are essentially regarding terminology and ritual—not theology. This is very important to know. So, if you are Protestant or Catholic, and this book or some chapter of it has touched your spirit to give yourself to God, just go ahead right now. Take advantage of the moment. And LIVE A VITAL NEW ENRICHING GOD LIFE!

See how that very special power of God through His Holy Spirit will change you. That change can be described only as rebirth and re-creation! The change comes when a person loves Jesus and allows Jesus into his or her heart. At that very moment you will experience forgiveness for the past. You will be armed with the Holy Spirit for the future. You will wholeheartedly accept and surrender to the will of God in your existence. And through the appropriate baptism, as stated in St. John's Gospel, of

Spirit and water you will become citizens of the Kingdom. That right is ours by inheritance.

"I tell you most solemnly, unless a man is born through water and the Spirit, he cannot enter the Kingdom of God." (John 3:5)

22.
The Great Earthquake

Jesus clashed with the religious authorities. The friction could not be avoided. The collision was shocking, inhuman; it ended in deicide. Jesus was condemned; the God-man was hurled upon the Cross. Nails were driven through His hands and feet; a lance speared His side. Blood and water flowed forth. The Christ was dead. And from His wounded side the Church was born. Incredible! That which man can inflict is always incredible; but that which God can do is always *the miracle of life*. Because Jesus was a threat to the officials, there was only one thing they could do: get rid of Him.

The enemies of Jesus believed they had a victory. This Jesus would no longer be a threat to them and to all they stood for. His enemies that night were probably entertaining themselves. No doubt as they ate and drank they sighed with relief. They were snickering; they were laughing and chiding. "That was a close call—THAT JESUS! But we finally got him. He had a lot of friends. Imagine all those miracles! He claimed authority, did he? Well, we showed him where authority really lies. He even made us at times look stupid. But we *got* him. And this is the *end* of him!"

The world that witnessed man trying to put God to death could still hear echoing across the land Jesus' loud cry and gasp. And when the crucified Lord fell into the sleep of death, the world in which they had been living suddenly lost all its hopes and dreams. Everything suddenly turned bleak. An emptiness overwhelmed the hearts of Jesus' followers. What else was there to do but to go back home. Their hearts were like the tomb of Nicodemus which absorbed within its confines the corpse of Jesus. The stone was placed at the entrance. All had ended in disaster.

But was that really the end? God has no end. God is a God of promises. God is a God of life. Death has no hold on God. God in the flesh of Jesus Christ appears momentarily as loser, but in God's moment becomes the eternal victor!

It was Sunday morning. Something *happened!* And that which happened took everybody by surprise. What was happening before the very eyes of man was something beyond anything he could have humanly contrived or imagined. It was just totally impossible—absolutely incredible to the finite human mind. But it was real. It *changed* the lives of His disciples: their whole way of thinking, feeling, and acting. Whatever was happening, it certainly confused the enemies of the Lord!

It was the third day after the Crucifixion. It was Easter Sunday. But in the annals of history, this particular Sunday was to become THE MOST IMPORTANT DAY in the history of mankind: past, present, and to come. In the truth of Scripture, the event of events is recorded: "On the third day He was raised to life." Yes, THE TOMB IS EMPTY! The news spread like wildfire among the Christian communities. There circulated various accounts of how the tomb was found empty, how the Lord appeared to disciples on the road to Emmaus, how Jesus came through closed doors at the Cenacle and sat with His Apostles, how He astonished them when He ate with them, appeared at a lake, as well as many other incidents. Yes, Jesus was ALIVE!

The friends of Jesus were having a new religious experience of God. Attuned to the truth of this resurrection reality, the Apostles were growing in the power of a new meaning. They began to see themselves as Jesus prepared them to be: men with new convictions, new duties. They were to be fishers of men! And the Master was now finalizing their ambassadorship. He was about to send them as witnesses to these extraordinary experiences. Jesus really meant something to them NOW! Jesus cleared their minds about Himself, and He aided them now to think straight. The world was to become their parish. Going forth into every land created for mankind, these Apostles would proclaim the Good News: the Kingdom, the invitation, the surrender to the Lord, the ongoing witness of conversions.

I now invite you, the reader, to affirm your journey in strength and in power. Your successful power for Christian living must be founded upon the Resurrection. Without that, our life is totally empty and futile. Those who experienced the many apparitions of the risen Jesus were totally convinced of this fact. They in turn told of their personal encounter with the risen Lord. The strength of their Christian living, their Christian witnessing, derived only from that truth experienced by themselves. That is the power!

If you believe in me, as a minister of Divine Teaching, Healing, and Love, it is because you believe in God! And so you see, you do have faith; and your faith is built upon a reason. That reason is the authority of the

Risen Christ. The Risen Christ lives in His Church. Jesus has not left us as orphans. He has promised to be with us to the end. HE LIVES! Wrapped in a shroud, entombed between cold slabs, buried in a stranger's grave because He Himself was too poor to even make such burial provisions, Jesus has dispelled the curse of death. A tomb, a shroud, a grave, a stone could not make His earthly existence final. Death has no control over God! Satan working through evil people has no power through sickness, disease, destruction, and death over the Lord Jesus. Jesus is *not* Satan's prisoner. Nor are you when you stay close to the Lord.

Do you feel the joy of this resurrection? You can, if you really wish to. No matter what life has done to us, no matter how many promises life has made, no matter how many promises life has broken, the only truth that counts is that the *Resurrection of Jesus is your joy, as it is His joyful victory!* This victorious glory of Jesus is your Christian hope! Sickness, disease, death—this is not an end for you! It is NOT an END for US! Christ has conquered!

But do you really *believe* He is alive? Do you honestly accept this story? You say that your faith tells you so; but still you would like to have a reason for your faith. And that is good! We *do* have reason for believing. Think about it.

Faith, according to Scripture, is "believing in something we cannot prove." But it is not believing in something without reason. You have, I have faith not because we have proof, but because we have *reasons;* and our reasons are the Word of God! Scripture and Tradition are powerful means of proof, but they flow from the Church. When Jesus established His Church, when Jesus sent His Apostles out to establish in the hearts of every human being the Kingdom of God, He did so without having had such wonderful publishing companies. He gave His Apostles a command! Go and teach and preach all that I have given you: this was the essence of faithful ambassadorship. Neither Scripture nor Tradition is the sole rule of faith. The rule of faith is that norm that determines our faith, namely, the reason why you and I believe. Inasmuch as your faith, my faith, must conform with the contents of Scripture and Tradition, these two sources must be called rules of faith. So strictly speaking, this rule of faith is only that by which our understanding of the Scriptures and Tradition is determined. The Scripture alone, as beautiful and powerful as it is, cannot be this ruling principle. The same applies to Tradition, taken apart from the living teaching duty of the Church. It is certain that God has delivered the Scriptures to the Church with the intention that they should be read and used as one of the sources of faith.

There also exists in the Church, as different from the Scriptures, a tradition of divinely revealed doctrines and institutions. Tradition in its strictest definition means a *transmission* of the truths of salvation (the Kingdom of God at hand). These transmitted truths of salvation are: the NEW BIRTH EXPERIENCE (conversion) and the BAPTISM OF THE HOLY SPIRIT (the Pentecostal Experience). Both experiences, to be authentic and valid, must be discerned and protected by the SOLE RULE OF FAITH, namely, *the teaching authority of the Church.* Without this teaching authority of the Church, there cannot be the protective hand of infallibility protecting and guiding God's people to the Kingdom of God. And so, tradition is nothing more than a transmission of revealed truths or beliefs handed down either orally or through inspired writings. Holy Scripture alone, therefore, does not remain as the only fundamental rule of faith. Scripture itself, especially that of the New Testament, has been compiled from the oral tradition of the Church—namely, the teaching and the preaching commission of Jesus Christ to His Apostles: Mark 16:15 says, "Go out to the whole world; proclaim the Good News to all creation." Be sure, therefore, that you understand that we are here speaking not of apostolic or ecclesiastical traditions as such, but of *those that trace their origin from Christ Himself and the Holy Spirit!*

And so, our faith *is* exciting when we know why we believe. *"O FELIX CULPA,* O HAPPY FAULT," we sing at the Saturday Easter Vigil. Christ has come, Christ has conquered, Christ reigns forever VICTOR!

23.
We Have Seen . . .
and Believe

Do you become excited and enthused when you read the Acts of the Apostles? It really is a very simple narrative of the Church's early dealings. It followed immediately after Jesus' Ascension. Acts 4:29–30 almost makes one's blood bubble with fire and love and zeal! It records "enable thy servants to preach thy word confidently, by stretching out thy Hand to heal; and let signs and miracles be performed by the name of Jesus, thy holy Son." (Knox)

Pentecost cost God something: it cost Him His son, Jesus. The Crucifixion with its Friday, which became GOOD for you and me, ended not with the finish of God on earth, but in the *beginning of new life through the Resurrection.* When the Pentecost of that year occurred, three thousand people heard a Gospel message from Peter and the Apostles (Acts 2). One powerful sermon—filled with truth. Can you imagine what it was to hear that one sermon? That one simple message converted three thousand listeners. It was only fifty-two days after Jesus had been put to the Cross and buried in the tomb. But the converts to Christ through the service testimony of the first Apostles indicates that they had to have been *absolutely certain that the Lord was risen in truth.* These converts were not afraid of the authorities, the persecutors, of possible personal imprisonment, or of death itself. They were in Jerusalem at the time of their conversions just a few hundred yards from Calvary's hill and the nearby tomb.

As they witnessed Jesus risen, they themselves had a New Risen Spirit. Jesus breathed upon them; and He gave them THE NEW BIRTH! Forty days from then, He would personally baptize them in His own Holy Spirit. Because of this experience they were now absolutely certain of the Master being alive. They were fearless. During the past three years they had been only disciples of inquiry, curiosity perhaps, students in the Divine School of Learning. But now! They became Apostles of Service. They had a mission! No more "identity crisis." They knew where they were going and wasted no time.

The Divine Mission of Christ, then, is proved dramatically and force-fully by His Resurrection from the dead. It is both a miracle and a fulfillment of prophecy. It is the foundation of our faith. It is *fact*. It is affirmed by the most reliable witnesses. The disciples of Christ preached the Resurrection before the world. Their truthfulness and sincerity are manifested in their whole conduct. They foresaw and soon experienced that their preaching the Resurrection of our Lord would inevitably lead to persecution. It would even send them to death. Even if they had wished to, they could not deceive. It would have been impossible to concoct a plan in so short a time amid all the confusion. Even if they thought of doing so, there was always the immediate possibility of being betrayed by some of the many accomplices.

The disciples, you must remember, had personally witnessed the atro-cious Crucifixion. And when they had seen their Master destroyed, their dreams shattered. From the very early hours of Holy Thursday supper all they were experiencing was sadness, melancholy, discouragement, and fright. Their hearts and minds were hardly receptive for the incredible. They were not thinking of any type of resurrection, that's for sure! They sneered at the women's reports, calling them tales of utter womanly delusion. But to Mary Magdalene, the Resurrection was no delusion! She KNEW WHAT SHE SAW! SHE KNEW WHOM SHE EXCITEDLY TOUCHED in her moment of overwhelming joy! For both of them, for Jesus and her, life had taken on a sacred tenderness, a new and strangely beautiful meaning. When the Blessed Lord stood and looked down in Mary Magdalene's wide-opened, astonished eyes, her heart sang within her. And at her first touch of Him—alive—she experienced once again boundless happiness.

The circumstances under which Christ appeared after the Resurrection prove that the disciples themselves were not deceived. Jesus did not ap-pear to only a few, but to many; even to "more than five hundred of the brothers at the same time." (1 Cor. 15:6) The Lord appeared not only once, but repeatedly during forty days. He appeared not only in the darkness of the night, but also in the light of day. Jesus ate with them. He showed them His honorable scars—the prints of His wounds. He even commanded Thomas, one of the disciples, to touch them. They were not overcredulous either; the report of the women did at first appear to them as idle tales. (Luke 24:11) Then, too, they hardly trusted their own eyes. (Luke 24:37) And even those who were convinced by obvious proofs could find no credence with their brethren. (Mark 16:13)

Another confirming proof is that the murderers of Christ are witnesses to His Resurrection. Their behavior with the Roman guards was out of order. They insisted upon the soldiers being tried and severely punished; they bribed them to admit that while they were asleep the disciples of Jesus had stolen the body. It is interesting that eight years after the fact, St. Matthew, before Jews and Romans, asserted this without fear of contradiction. (Matt. 28:13) Astonishing how evil contradicts itself! These murderers of Christ rendered the same behavior toward the disciples as they had to the Roman officials. Instead of inflicting punishment upon the disciples for this pretended crime, they merely imposed silence on them. (Acts 4:18)

Finally, the entire world, by its faith in the Resurrection, bears witness to the same fact. Just a few weeks after the Resurrection, the Apostles preached the Resurrection and, as mentioned before, the three thousand people professed their faith in the Resurrection. Other believers, even indirect witnesses to the Divine Mission of Jesus, increased from day to day.

Was the Resurrection a REAL MIRACLE? If it was, then that too is proof. If a certain miracle is at all possible, the event in question must be construed to be such. It evidently leaves no room for reasonable or well-grounded doubt, but only for an unreasonable and groundless doubt. The Resurrection is evidently a miracle, because it could not be effected by any created natural force. It had to be accomplished only by Divine Force.

The resurrection of a dead person—that is, the reunion of his soul with the body—is beyond human power. And even more so, how could any human activity that can be exerted directly on the physical *body* have power to recall a departed soul to its abandoned tenement? Not even spirits, good or evil, raise the dead to life. For they have no power to withdraw the souls from the reward or punishment apportioned to them by God at their departure from life. They just don't have that power to put departed souls back into this worldly state of probation. Certainly, not even the evil spirits can do this because they possess no authority over the souls of the blessed who are entirely in the arms of God. Even the good angels with all their power are only instruments of God, who is Himself the chief agent.

One of the most exacting proofs of faith is that of martyrdom. The fortitude displayed by the martyrs is a miracle of the moral order produced only by the grace of God. It serves also as an evidence of the

Divine Origin of Christianity, and consequently, of the truth of those supernatural facts on which it rests. It forms part of the Church's powerful teaching and preaching. It does not matter whether the martyrs died for the truth of the Christian religion itself, or for some particular dogma, or some Christian virtue. The fact is that they died, in any case, for Christianity. Nor does it matter if they died during an earlier age or a later age. The evidence is taken from the fortitude of the martyrs themselves and not from their formal testimony to particular facts. History cannot close its eyes and mind to the objective truth to which an extraordinary number of martyrs testified.

Men, women, and children, the young and the old, the rich and the poor, do not patiently submit to suffering, torture, and ignominious death without some powerful motive. This powerful motive must be either a natural or a supernatural one. In the case of the Christian martyrs it was not a natural motive founded upon natural causes, but a supernatural, extraordinary, marvelous effect of grace. The martyrs themselves declared that they were willing to die for Christ, and that this power was a strength from on high by which they were courageously able to endure their torture. Even the pagans themselves could not grasp how such men and women could suffer the atrocious pains. They stated that some power other than human was hovering over these Christians. Much more forcibly do the pagans profess this conviction by the fact that, influenced by the marvelous constancy of the martyrs, they themselves ultimately embraced Christianity.

The victory and the constancy of the martyrs was not inspired or motivated by vainglory, because among them were many who were not sensible to this motive. Some were little children, slaves, and men and women of the lowest rank. Many died exactly as they had lived: unknown. Their names are not even recorded. Nor did they accept death because of the possibility of some religious veneration. Many of them knew that they could never receive honor since their own names and their resting places were quite unknown. At that time there were so many martyrs, it often happened that death for the faith received little notice. Nor were they motivated by selfish reasons, such as the hope of a happy eternity. True, they had the prospect of an eternal reward; but it was a supernatural motive: being in union with the grace of God sustained them. This hope alone, as a mere natural motive, could not produce in them such extraordinary fortitude because the goods that were promised them were of the spiritual order. They were not apt to meet temporal needs. It had to be only the grace of God!

And finally, it was not fanaticism! Fanaticism usually involves intensifying the means and (sometimes) forgetting the cause. It inevitably urges and leads to action and combat. Even if at times it enables some to bear extraordinary hardship, it eventually betrays a tendency to seek admiration. A fanatical person always displays deeper inordinate passions: he or she is deprived of self-possession. Fanaticism is only a mood. It produces morbid thrills. But it is short-lived. The martyrs, however, demonstrated constant, calm self-possession. As they maintained it, they showed how far removed they were from any kind of fanaticism.

It is evident that this miracle that we behold in the fortitude of the martyrs furnishes the utmost proof that our Blessed Lord was resurrected from the dead. It had to be a miracle of God because God would not encourage the faithful to persevere in a false religion. We must conclude, therefore, that God, by working this miracle in Christ and in those who believe in it, by working this miracle in the lives of His servants, has borne testimony to the truth of Christianity. And for this reason, the supernatural facts that are taught, preached, lived by, and written about, are to be adhered to.

We need to enter frequently into ourselves. We need to know our souls; to recognize their conditions in the light of faith, of eternity! We can find light in moments of darkness. We are not to lead God's People behind closed doors! We are *to stand steadfast!* Christ is the same yesterday, today, and always!

We can pray and search the tombs of our broken humanity. But we should not end there. We need to kneel before the Lord. Like Magdalene and the Apostles, like his disciples, we can raise our tear-stained eyes. We can hear a voice: He is not dead. HE IS RISEN. Alleluia!

24.

There Is Always a Special Road
for Everyone's Journey

There will forever be—for every man, woman, and child—a road that will lead in journey. It is a very personal road. It often tests our frustration tolerance. It is the crossroad of decision. Without it, one can, in the contemporary jargon, "crack up." It desperately needs to be confronted. Our survival depends upon it. IT IS THE MOMENT OF TRUTH!

Are you at that moment in your life? It has to come sooner or later. Regardless of who or what a person is, becomes, or hopes to be, such a person will inevitably face that moment, encounter that crossroad, make that journey. It is a road of decision only because it is a road paved by deliberation. If one is courageous, one will ultimately find that that road climaxes in a promised rainbow. To vacillate, to fear the encounter of new responsibilities for decision making, to deviate from the only clear possible road, is to be afraid of *facing life.* Like the puzzled Apostles after the Crucifixion, we forget that God's concern for us never dies.

Wouldn't it make a tremendous difference, offer the miracle for a better tomorrow, if one possessed the constant friendship of the Lord? If we had Jesus' never-ending help? Jesus—as only Jesus knows how—would demonstratively prove to you that He is your only source, that He alone can strengthen you, that He alone can wipe away your precious human tears. He alone can comfort your precious human hurts. Jesus alone can do all this—and *even more*—as He alone knows how to *cleanse you,* to *empower you* for greater service to yourself, your neighbor, your country, and the whole universe!

If in your hands you could hold the road map as planned by God for you, the honor, the splendor, the joy that the Almighty would bestow upon you would leave you awestruck, positively mesmerized! In every person's life, the *best is yet to be if we let God have His way.* And that is precisely what you will realize.

Do you allow God to be your companion? I mean really be your *friend* in every section, every emotion of your precious life? Do you allow Him to allow you to find Jesus in His true love? It is that true love that drew Him to His disciples after the Resurrection, even though they had deserted Him during His bitter Passion, during the very crucial hour of His Crucifixion. And just as our Dear Lord searched for His wandering disciples and Apostles so long ago, now as then He seeks you and me, He searches for everyone who like weak friends of old might be filled with doubts and questions, suffering and disappointment. Are you perhaps one of those who is not fully able to grasp the meaning and the ways of God acting in your life? Are there times when you can see nothing but *meaninglessness* in your existence? The poet Gilbert once penned similar thoughts as to God's companionship in our lives:

> When God is our Companion,
> As we walk the road of life,
> There is help for every problem
> And grace for care and strife!
> And we'll find that we've been happy
> All along the path we've trod,
> When in faith we've made the journey
> Hand-in-hand along with God!

ARE YOU ON THE ROAD THAT LEADS FROM THE TOMB?

And so, we must believe that the Lord Jesus is walking with us, and He will show us His closeness, and the purpose of our path. When we lose vision, we merely wander and meander through the night without a star. But with vision, we will come out from the darkness of the night.

In each human voyage of discovery there inevitably comes that one special encounter with the Hidden Countenance of the Resurrected Jesus. This experience is a repeat of that first experience of the glory of God, the Son Resurrected, and the discovery of oneself born afresh in the power of His appearance. This experience, for you and me, is the road to Emmaus. That road to Emmaus, though topographically only seven miles from Jerusalem, is that road that winds through the human soul, from Calvary to the nearby stranger's tomb, from the empty tomb to the inn at Emmaus.

St. Paul, as he writes to the Romans, indicates that Jesus made His love real to you, to me. What Paul is showing is that in practice our Blessed Lord stood for something that cost Him His life. So much of the Gospels are concerned with this event. You may at times disagree as much as you wish about certain moral and disciplinary issues, but in the end all that counts is what you think about Jesus. That will make the difference!

If you want to find your star that heralds a new birth, you need to find that wisdom of the crib that leads to the strength of the Cross. The Crucifixion would have been a disaster, a tragedy of death, if there were no faith, no Resurrection! The empty tomb does not prove anything to us except the fact that a dead body was laid there, and that at another time —a few days later—the body was not there. The empty tomb did not convince Jesus' friends that He had been raised. *That which convinced His friends that Jesus had risen was THE NEW RELIGIOUS EXPERI-ENCE OF GOD which Jesus made possible.*

No one really knows, except God and you, the enormous price you have paid—and still pay—in life, trying to be *all that God wants you to be.* Only God and you know how hard it has been, and is, living in today's age. Some of you are weary, even burned out. Some of you are frequently brought very close to tears. You've experienced emotional let-downs; you've suffered for right against wrong; you've borne the Cross with the suffering Jesus of Nazareth. You've been told that the tomb is empty but your momentary enthusiasm fades—it is not gone, but it is faded. You feel entombed yourself. What you need is a resurrection of the dead bones, a resurrection of faith—faith that Jesus is alive for *you.*

Our Blessed Lord is waiting—until the end of time—for you, for me, for all people, to have faith in Him. He continuously knocks. He patiently awaits our voices saying: "Come in. Stay with us, Lord; it is getting late." He yearns to give you this new encounter with Him, the living resurrected Lord, who is present in our midst and from whom we derive our daily strength. The Risen Christ has a new appearance just for you. Where will you find Him?

25.
The Road to Emmaus and You

The experience of our barrenness is painful. But it is the Lord's visitations that can turn our barrenness into fruitfulness, our painfulness into delight. Barrenness is stripping. The great stripping took place on Calvary's heights. Perhaps in your barrenness you can bring your desolation and your poverty to His fruitful resurrection power. When you come to the realization of your barrenness, you are on the road to humility. Humility is strength, and God can use only a humble person, a broken person, a weak person, a person weeping copiously, a person wholeheartedly repentant. God allows such a chosen soul to appear loathesome—without fruitfulness—but He does so only to soon cover such a chosen disciple with clusters of precious grapevines from whence there can flow forth new wine. Yes! A sense of our personal poverty has the force to drive us to the Lord. And without any shadow of a doubt, there is where you and I—everyone—need to be.

Every person at one time or another, in fact many times, has had to experience some sort of death, some sort of severance, some sort of breaking from oneself, from another, so as to fructify in the glory a new maturity. This is *RESURRECTION LIFE.* This is the Resurrection Life that Jesus had when He came forth from the grave. Barrenness is not final when we live and die with Jesus. What Jesus did to His humanity for you and for me, He will continue to do in a very personal and extraordinary way. In Jesus' lifetime, all sorts of observers, but especially His nearest friends, recognized Him as more than just an *ordinary person.* Jesus always projected some magnetic force that commanded people's respect, even loyalty and love. To everyone, friend and foe, He was puzzling; people did not know what to make of Him. All that could be seen was that He definitely stood for something. And that something was God's road to the Kingdom. With every word and deed, Jesus was making it crystal clear that God was making Himself visible through Jesus Himself. The Master's message was the Gospel truth about His father, our God. And it spoke *openly*—regardless of opposition—about persons, their salvation, and the world they lived in.

Without the truth of the Resurrection you will remain barren. Without the acceptance of the Resurrection you will remain in your life entombed. With your total unreserved embrace, your hugging so to speak, of the resurrected Jesus, you will be elated to realize that *human death is not final.*

I have repeatedly attempted to impress upon you the strength indwelling within the power of the Resurrection, similar to the bubbling forces of a volcano seeking its release through eruption. Nature will claim in time its release for life as it does with everything. Nature is on God's side. And so it is my hope, my desire and my prayer, that the truth of the Resurrection did something to you. You should have perceived that *a Living Christ* enables you to face barrenness, emptiness, and death. The thought of death is not appealing to anybody. It's gloomy. We even live as if it won't happen. But we really know differently, don't we? Inevitably we must face death. However, for the believer in the resurrected Jesus death is not morose. It isn't even tragic! That Master's victory over death is our pledge as well. Jesus confirmed this emphatically: ". . . because I live and you will live." (John 14:19)

And so, if you really believe in His Resurrection, then death is a defeated enemy, and it does not have any power. When, in its human form, it does occur, *it will be the road of your human journey passing through the gateway of eternal life.*

Until that victorious moment, however, every wandering soul—every Christian—needs to keep his vision of the Easter Dawn! The Lord's Resurrection becomes more than an extraordinary occurrence of the first century; it belongs to the ages! No matter how much we study it, we remain baffled—or experience restlessness by the Christ knocking on the human soul. That sensitizing knock will point us on the road that takes us to conversion. It challenges the philosopher who seeks "explanation." It perplexes the historian who seeks "reproduction." It perpetually defies time which attempts "to erase." But to those with FAITH, ah, it continues to say: "Receive Me . . . I am He whom thou seekest." Because of His death and Resurrection, you and I are now able to know, experience, and avail ourselves of the joys of sins forgiven; and we have the assurance of really going to heaven when we must leave this life. Jesus said to Martha: "I am the resurrection. If anyone believes in me, even though he dies he will live." (John 11:25)

God is using this chapter to touch your soul. He is offering you something much more: if you are good, you will be better; if you are better, you can become *the best.* If you are neither, then you are ready to walk the road to GOOD! What greater confirmation could be added to your hope than the repeated, poignant statements found in the Acts of the Apostles. Over and over again, the Apostles continue to speak the Gospel as centering in the death, burial, and Resurrection of Jesus. They emphasize the solemn command of the Master that all who would follow His teaching and share His life, must die to sin through repentance, be buried in the waters of baptism for the remission of their sins in the name of the Father, the Son, and the Holy Spirit, *and be raised to walk in the newness of a life completely dedicated to the service of Jesus.* Each time a person gives his life to Christ, the death, burial, and Resurrection of Jesus are reenacted.

Easter is for YOU! "Unless a wheat grain falls on the ground and die, it remains only a single grain; but if it dies, it yields a rich harvest." (John 12:24) Easter for you is a time for new life! Anything that was in you, or still is in you if you have not yet surrendered it, can be put to death, and a new life can spring forth. Anything of darkness can go out of you. A warm sun wants to shine in. Give God a chance, and life for you will have a new meaning. These deeply significant thoughts were spoken by our Lord Jesus to the crowds in Jerusalem just a few days before the authorities convicted Him of blasphemy. To some of His listeners these thoughts may have seemed no more than a simple declaration of nature's law of death and resurrection. But they were clearly prophetic of Christ's own terrible fate, of His rising from the tomb, and more especially, of His ever-broadening influence over mankind's behavior. For just as a grain of seed is buried in the soil before it is gathered in harvest time, so it was for Jesus.

What road are you really traveling? In whose footsteps are you walking? Where are you going? Without faith, hope would have little meaning. Are you losing your hope for living? This whole book is meant to rekindle a fire within you *to hope for a better tomorrow.*

Let us share one more story, about a shattered hope caused by vacillating faith. It is a beautiful story: simple in its narrative, but filled with understanding, compassion, resurrection, exciting adventure. It has been preserved for you and me in the Scriptures. (cf. Luke 24:15–35.) Come now and make this journey with the two disciples on the road to Emmaus. Walk with them; feel their pain; experience their doubts. With Jesus, walk with them and "talk that walk." Be as they; share your momentary problems. Listen and learn from the Lord. See how these disciples, after they returned to Jerusalem, were all aglow and renewed in their faith. Imagine their conversation.

We saw Him on the road to Emmaus. He looked like any other stranger. Perhaps we could have recognized Him sooner if we had not been in a deep state of depression. But then, as we now look back, we see depression is more often than not just that which blinds us to the sight of God. How downcast we were. Our faces were weighed, and furrows could be seen. We felt so let down! But then this stranger— suddenly not there and NOW THERE—startled us. His words and questions startled us even more when He asked what matters we were discussing. We stopped short. Was it possible that there was someone who knew nothing about this Jesus of Nazareth?

And as we told Him the story of this Jesus of Nazareth, He seemed to perceive deeper wounds within us. His questions were really pene- trating, and resurrecting from us in our answers our buried faith. That was a good approach, now that we look back at that glorious moment. Jesus was really with us. We guess that in human hearts, so depressed as ours were, there is no human pain more sorrowful than that of lost hope. We had hoped once but now we felt let down.

It seems that He read our pain clearly; He diagnosed it well. When one loses love, he sins. When one loses faith, he rankles. When one loses hope, he dies. But repentance and rededication can bring new life. And that is what Jesus was doing with us. He aided us to repent of our doubt and find love again. He aided us to find faith again by experienc- ing Him in real faith. When we did that, our HOPE WAS RESUR- RECTED. The girls of the town, His favorite followers, are now trying to say that He is alive. They can't find Him around the tomb. So we have had enough. It was time for some fresh air, and so here we are on this road!

Thank God for the gift of life as well as for supportive friendship. We all need to sustain one another at some time—whether you to me or I to you. And herein is one blessed moment where you and I are able to rise again and again, afresh and afresh, in revitalized purpose, in constancy of service, in the joy of new life. The work Our Lord gives us, our special ministry of service in His name, is called an apostolate. If we are willing to live and to serve fruitfully, and not be barren with our life, then it is of paramount importance that we *know* from where our strength and pur- pose come; that source of life is *the soul of our apostolate.*

Just like every other human being you too have a very special personal mission to fulfill. It must not be fruitless! You must strive so that it will not be barren! I entreat you to grasp this fully. As a follower of the resurrected Christ, having this new experience of God, you cannot just simply be a follower of Jesus; once you've experienced His countenance you must be a doer for Jesus.

Let us try to understand others, learn their points of view. Let us assist others to seek and find the Truth. Let us guide them—as we have—to hear Jesus' RISEN VOICE so that they too come to know that they are not left silent. Let us be other Good Shepherds and gather the strays into the flock. *No one should walk the road to Emmaus alone!*

PART VI
The Healing of
a Nation

26.
God's Tears for His World

Man's broken brotherhood is God's wound. God's tears for His world is a real portrayal of the love of God in search of His lost and straying children. Man may be in search of his own destiny, but God, as the Hound of Heaven, follows His creature man until man either accepts His authentic destiny or rejects the author of such a destiny. With every new age, there is a further step away from that historic moment when God not only spoke His Word of concern, but sent forth that Word to be visibly seen, touched, experienced. He sent His Divine Son, Jesus, the Christ, the Messiah, the Savior. This Jesus has attempted time and time again, century after century, with individuals and with groups of individuals incorporated into nations, to factualize the parable He told of the Prodigal Son returning to his former, intended status. The story speaks the thoughts of Jesus: "So he left the place and went back to his father. While he was still a long way off, his father saw him and was moved with pity. He ran to the boy, clasped him in his arms, and kissed him tenderly." (Luke 15:20)

God's tears for His world are tears of His authentic and never-ending love. The world progresses step-by-step. With each new generation, the veil of past generations is lifted. Another world appears: tossing waves of all sorts in philosophies, sociologies, the occult, and a multitude of "isms." Active demonic forces are not stilled, nor are they stifled. They come in many deceptive forms, producing in us the experience of depression, anger, and lack of self-contentment. The devil never can be accused as "a false promiser." He stays "true" to his cunning enticement. He delivers what he temporarily promises. But that is as far as it goes. Eternity of happiness with God—our ultimate and joyful purpose—the devil cannot grant. He himself and all his demons in cohort are eternally damned. Absolutely no end. In eternity there are no reruns, no second chance! But God, who is absolutely in love with His creature man, will send forth with more might than Satan can, forces of good to combat the forces of evil. The devil will always attempt to counteract that heavenly force of God's love for us: the outpouring of the Holy Spirit. Holy angels are sent forth as armies; their mighty power represents the ever-present, saving love of God.

With every soul that is lost to Satan's wiles, with every nation that is destroyed by the hand of the Evil One through poverty, plunder, war, destruction, pestilence, we are given a glimpse of how ugly Satan and sin really are. And at the same time, we can look up to God and experience a glimpse into His heart, filled with grief over the fate of a world that He created out of His abundant love and goodness. Tearfully, after experiencing the woes of sin—brokenness, depersonalization, separation from true love, goodness, godliness—each impoverished, repentant person, broken from life's years yet loyal to faith and decency, will perceive the Divine Relentless Lover. Poignant and compelling, His loving pleas and lamenting come across with almost irresistible force. Yes, God has tears for His world. The world is His wound. We cannot flee; we cannot ignore that cry.

27.

America, a Land of Heritage

Every nation is a massive mosaic of heritage. Take Jerusalem, for example. As one visits and views this ancient city, one not only feeds his senses and mind, but one also penetrates a deep history. Jerusalem not only stands amid the poor Judean Hills, but in the eyes of the Divine Creator, this city is a special city: it was chosen by God. Because of that choice, that nation was destined to be the bulwark of monotheism. Every nation has its own individualistic destiny. God makes nothing for nothing's sake. This chosen city of Jerusalem is considered *the* sacred city for half the human race; it is the religious capital of the three monotheistic faiths. During my stay in Jerusalem in August 1984, I personally witnessed these three faiths in the staunchness of their adherence to religious observance. God had a plan for Jerusalem, as He has a plan for every tribe and nation.

For the Jews, Jerusalem is the symbol of their past victories, their historic glories, and even the hope for the future. Christians too look devotedly upon this ancient city—torn asunder so often, pillaged and tossed from one national command to another, age after age. There have been more battles fought at those Jerusalem walls than at any other battlefield in the world. For the Christians it is the city made holy by the sandled feet of Jesus. It was his mission field. He preached, taught, and died there. It was a land designated for honor and destiny if only that land with its leaders, be they religious or civic, and all its people, would listen and be faithful to the Lord; if only both its leaders and people would recognize their follies and failures, repent from their evil ways, and humbly fall upon their knees in prayer and rededicate themselves to the Lord. If they would only do this—as every nation should—God would heal the land. The book of Chronicles exhorts the nations: "If my people will humble themselves and pray, and search for me, and turn from their wicked ways, I will hear them from heaven and forgive their sins and heal their land. For I have chosen this temple and sanctified it to be my home forever; my eyes and my heart shall always be here." (2 Chron. 7:14, 16) (LB)

God loves His People. God gathers His people into families, cities, nations. The book of Revelation predicts that one day men and women from every tribe, tongue, and nation will stand before Him. As people recognized their need to survive, to march onward to some "Great Expectation," they grouped together. A distinctive feature of such grouping was their unity of enterprise and understanding, and their dependency upon Almighty God. With such conscious dependency upon Divine Providence they knew that victory would be theirs.

America is a land of heritage, too. It is our land. Let it be loved by every man, woman, and child. Let every immigrant who dares to enter its shores look up to it as a country willing to give of itself unreservedly—but only to those who gift themselves to the land. The gift of self to one's country is the greatest and most precious surrender of apostolic maturity. When a person reaches the degree of union with God—keeping God resurrected and alive within one's own existence—and has not evaded the "gift of self," then there will continue to burn the flame of zeal.

In the National Archives building in Washington, D.C., there is a historic testimony to American growth. It reads: "The heritage of the past is the seed that brings forth the harvest of the future." Our land is a country of people who have worked together. They labored for a common unified goal. They lived, survived, worked, fought, and even died for that dream. They had a destiny. They knew America had a fate, a fate planned by God. It would benefit not only itself, but all nations. America was given them by God as a shining land. It was not a land to be pillaged or polluted. America to these pioneers was not a land to be betrayed from light into darkness, which at times is the fate of many nations. Darkness must not settle on these sacred shores! Men experience this darkness; they know it by name: hate, greed, bigotry, crime, hunger, despair, evil, madness, violence. In its final analysis, all of these are only symptoms of the central disorder, *a wasting of the spirit!*

Youngest of the great nations of the world, America, in the palms of her Creator, held out her arms to the wounded and the hurt, to the world's distressed. Men and women of every age were proud to be her sons and daughters. Citizenship was a noble and distinctive status. Citizenship, moreover, was a badge of valiant heroism. Patriotism itself was a very valorous medal of manhood and womanhood. As eyes looked across its terrain—plains and valleys, mountains and streams—they envisioned a spreading land of plenty crowned with beauty. America—especially the United States—was a dream of human brotherhood. Its nascent spirit awakened a reality! But most of all, the United States of America was *her people!*

Yes. Those archives speak well. Look back to the days when our nation of the United States was young. There you'll find story after story of people working unselfishly together. They cleared forests, built cabins, and reaped harvests. Those pioneers did many things together that they could not do alone.

But they were not loners. They were a unit. They were a family of people. History records them not just as individuals who worked, but a *people grouped together* who worked. As groups, villages, towns, counties, states—all of them labored and toiled together to help build a great country. But when at times discord arose and groups lost sight of their faith and their moral goals, they worked *against* one another. And the nation suffered. The love of freedom that encompassed this land suddenly gave way to disruption. The true faith in freedom gifted them by God was overshadowed by tyranny; degradation and brutality replaced discipline. Something happened to its people. They turned against each other. The American states became divided. Neighbors became strangers; and some even became enemies. The wasting spirit of oppression against neighbors left a historical scar. America, and the United States, became awfully cruel. Dissatisfaction from within eventually spews itself upon the land. There is violence caused by envy, jealousy, and hate. Like unbridled stallions, totally unrestrained, the people became egocentric, selfish, spurning all dogmatic and moral codes, lusting after material gain and profit. The law, for that reason, had to go. They scorned both religious and civic ordinances and America became lawless. Some called it insanity. Indeed, it was insanity! All evil is insane. Some of the chosen leaders and many of the citizens of this vast wonderful land had turned away from reason. The land America became polluted. Greed and avarice, emotions which we all possess ran wild! Pursuit of profit replaced that of honor. America became despised and carried its face in shame. Men died who, right or wrong, claimed the right to speak freely, the right to think, to write, to pray as their good conscience warranted. Truth walked away, because it was ignored. America became sick. Its people's spirit ailed.

What's wrong with the world? What's wrong with the land? Where are the noble answers to be found? What has been forgotten? Where has the nation, the world been wandering? A correspondent for the London *Times* once did a series of articles attempting to explore the problems of the world. As he ended each article, he repeatedly asked one question: "What's wrong with the world?" G. K. Chesterton had a reply: "I AM!"

The healing of our nation—or any nation for that matter—will require the ultimate supreme sacrifice: to fall once again upon its knees and pray. The failures of government and the social and sociopathological evils in recent years have not been so much the failures of institutions. They are basically the failures of people. Whether or not one tries to deny God and His moral code for living, the truth remains that there is a God. This is His world, and it must be directed according to His plans of governance. When nature is abused, as for example, through slavery, the natural law is not upheld. Natural law says that each of us is a freely endowed *person.* And so, in the case of slavery, nature will rebel, retaliate, rectify, justify its created purpose. God told the children of Israel that righteousness exalts a nation, and sin is a reproach to any people. And this righteousness comes to us only through His Son, Jesus Christ.

The classic American philosophy is that material growth and scientific and technological change are the keys to a better life. This is like wanting the wine without the container. God loves His people. God wants His people. God will be forced through His love and mercy to lead humanity back to itself through its own brokenness. If He must begin with sin and evil, then—as He did with Mary Magdalene or with the thief who repented at that eleventh hour—He will begin there. He will turn evil into a pathway for rectifying a repentant nation, a nation on its knees, so that it may humbly look up and cry out, "Save us, O Lord, save us lest we perish!"

People have been betrayed by a host of things. Materialism has not paid off. Secularism and humanism have been deceitful. Promises have not been fulfilled. The people have been betrayed by time-serving politicians, pietistic and sanctimonious clerics, whose bearing and words of prayer lack soul. Man has made himself a stranger to his God. He has forgotten that his true home is on far distant shores.

Values! Where have they gone? Erroneous ideas are being questioned now by the very ones who are hurting and wounded. But through our wounds we can be healed. The old faith in human progress is being challenged as never before. Even on the international scene today our world is learning that nations too must enter and look within their own selves *as a whole.* They must see themselves holistically: as a being with both material goods supplied by the state and spiritual goods provided by the Church. Though both state and Church have equal just rights, the spiritual goal of each person surpasses that of the temporal order. The state, the country, the nation have been naturally formed by man for his total material survival. The state was made for man, not man for the state. For world peace, therefore, nations too are seeking and learning intelligent ways and honorable means to work together. The ever-present threat of war is a grim reminder of what happens when nations pursue only their own selfish goals.

Must we let history repeat itself? Let there be war no more! Let there be hatred, envy, annihilation no more! Let human destruction both from within and without cease! NO MORE, NO MORE!

As each nation will humbly look up to that ultimate uncaused Cause, that Supreme Power, let it reflect on how great a nation it can become. Let each nation also reflect—and reflect seriously—that this contemporary age is no different in human essence and nature, in human outlook, as ages gone by. Only our scene is different. Our ways and means for growth or destruction are more sophisticated, more quick, more decisive.

History has made it abundantly clear not only in the lives of nations, but also in those of individuals, that those who by their lives and actions declare their independence from God soon become slavishly dependent upon the circumstances and changes of human existence. History also conclusively shows, on the other hand, that those individuals who constitute a people forming a nation are those who humbly declare their dependence upon God. And these are remarkably free and independent people.

28.
A Nation in Need of a New Birth

What our nation needs is a new birth! Slogans, clichés, and the like have always been part of our history—remember the New Deal, the New Frontier? Slogans are often used by political campaigners to garner votes. Some try to imitate old slogans; and since they are not original, the voter must be cautious. An imitator can be recognized as a fearful person, afraid that his or her ambition may be defeated. Such a person is not trustworthy.

Our history is filled with giants who walked honorably the halls of political fame. And we as Americans have the right to be humbly proud! Even nonpolitical figures have impacted on this great nation. Who does not remember Will Rogers (1879–1935)? What a sharp American humorist that cowboy/philosopher was! Through movies, books, radio, and newspaper columns, his salty political and social comments not only gained him popularity but stimulated the American people to think, to evaluate, to decide. One can almost hear his voice echo across the nation: "The difference between a politician and a statesman is that the politician thinks of the next election while the statesman thinks of the next generation."

Likewise, who has not been nourished and inspired by the great American politician from Salisbury (now Franklin), New Hampshire, the famous lawyer so well noted for his oratory, Daniel Webster (1782–1852). Indeed great were his deeds as was his echoing thunderous voice: "God grants liberty only to those who love it, and are always ready to guard and defend it."

Patrick Henry (1736–99) aroused the timid. His voice came alive with brilliant oratory while he served in the Virginia house of burgesses (1765–74) and the Continental Congress (1774–76), as well as during his governorship of Virginia (1776–79). His were not mere words. When he spoke people stood up and paid attention. They listened, they learned, they did something with their lives. He inspired them with his enthusiasm: "If this be treason, make the most of it." Especially notable was his speech in the Virginia convention of 1775: "Is life so dear, or peace so sweet, as to be purchased at the price of chains and slavery. Forbid it, Almighty God! I know not what course others may take, but as for me, give me liberty, or give me death!"

And here are still more words to inspire all Americans:

There is nothing wrong with America that faith, love of freedom, intelligence and energy of her citizens cannot cure.

DWIGHT D. EISENHOWER

Freedom of religion; freedom of the press, and freedom of person under the protection of the *habeas corpus.*

THOMAS JEFFERSON
in his First Inaugural Address

Stand fast therefore in the liberty wherewith Christ hast made us free, and be not entangled again with the yoke of bondage.

THOMAS PAINE in
"What Is the Constitution?"

It is by the goodness of God that in our country we have those three unspeakably precious things: freedom of speech, freedom of conscience and the prudence never to practise either of them.

MARK TWAIN in
"Following the Equator"

Moral courage is a rarer commodity than bravery in battle or great intelligence. Yet it is the one essential, vital quality for those who seek to change a world that yields most painfully the change.

SENATOR ROBERT F. KENNEDY in
To Seek a Newer World

The great inspiration—no doubt the greatest of them all—comes from the giant of presidents, Abraham Lincoln. Immortal are his words for any age. The following brief address embodied Lincoln's hopes for peace and reconstruction. The London *Times* called it "The most sublime State paper of the century." Lincoln himself commented positively about it when he wrote: "I expect (it) to wear as well as . . . perhaps better than anything I have produced, but I believe it is not immediately popular. Men are not flattered by being shown that there has been a difference of purpose between the Almighty and them. To deny it, however, in this case is to deny that there is a God governing the world . . ." The reference is to his Second Inaugural Address, delivered March 4, 1865. This is the closing part of it:

> Fondly do we hope, fervently do we pray, that this mighty scourge of war may speedily pass away. Yet if God wills that it continue until all the wealth piled by the bondsman's two hundred and fifty years of unrequited toil shall be sunk, and until every drop of blood drawn with the lash shall be paid by another drawn with the sword, as was said three thousand years ago, so still it must be said, "The judgments of the Lord are true and righteous altogether."
>
> With malice toward none, with charity for all, with firmness in the right, as God gives us to see the right, let us strive on to finish the work we are in, to bind up the nation's wounds, to care for him who shall have borne the battle, and for his widow, and his orphan—to do all which may achieve and cherish a just and lasting peace among ourselves and with all nations.

So, as we think again of the birth of our great nation, you and I can pray that our beloved country might have a new birth of freedom, a freedom built upon God and His commandments, apart from which any nation will perish. What our forefathers have done by word and sacrifice, we too can contribute to our nation's destiny. With their inspiration preceding us, we like them, and with God's blessings, can redeem our nation. Out of the greatness of the past we find the surest guide for the future. Lincoln's words enrich us with his overwhelming compassion: *"Let us bind up the nation's wounds."*

29.

And America Wept

There were shots fired in Maryland. A man is reported to have said, "It is sad," and he sighed. Another person said, "It should not happen," and he faded away. A third man said, "This is definitely wrong; it is absolutely wrong." And nobody did anything. Each one turned to other thoughts just as they had done with the scars of four presidential assassinations: Lincoln, Garfield, McKinley, and John F. Kennedy. All that America could do was to weep for its wounds.

History repeats itself: old moods with new labels, old attempts with new strategies. The atrocious assassinations, the ugly scene of love going sour, is nothing more than a repeat of the killing of the good man called Jesus. The day was Good Friday. The passion of hate was at work. An angry sky thundered in outward revolt and revenge upon the earth. Rocks split, and Calvary became a rock of ages. A funeral veil of utter darkness overshadowed the land, and the land was made desolate. A Black Friday was born for the first time in the history of the nascent Christian world. And yet, in spite of that terrible drastic day, the day on which Christ died in his humanity, *good sprang up.* Through the wisdom and mercy of the Almighty who will not be outdone in generosity, good always came out from evil.

Then too, there was the woman called Mary, the mother of Jesus, who became the prima donna, the first lady, the new Eve in the history of the world's salvation. Watch her as she cradled in her arms the limp body of her beloved Son. At that moment she became the Mother of Sorrows. As she gazed at the cold metal of the nails riveted by the executioners, as she saw and even touched the blood spilling so copiously upon her—from her waist to her feet as she held him in her arms beneath the Cross—she realized this was not Bethlehem with its joys, but that this was Calvary with its nails, blood, sweat, and tears. This was an assassination. And for the first time in her life she recognized herself to be the Mother of God's children, the Mother of the Victim Christ.

Such tragedy! Can there not be drawn an analogy of hope from Christ's dead body resting in his mother's lap, in a land of choice, Jerusalem? Can this country not be a repeat of a great nation called by God to experience its nourishment by the shedding of its leaders' blood, blood soaking the land? A land that is destined necessarily, it seems, must have its martyrs. In the memory of many of us who still live, we cannot forget that despicable act of our nation's own Black Friday, November 22, 1963. It was a crime akin to the one that happened on Calvary, this tragedy done to our country's commander and chief, John F. Kennedy, and his First Lady. Is it not significant that the United States, which is consecrated by God, should bear this tragedy of innocent blood? Was it not a blessing in disguise—this martyrdom in which the sands of our American soil were wetted with the blood of a Christian leader? Perhaps the message to the American people is that if a more lasting and holy good is to come to the United States—which has been so richly blessed by God—then we must experience again the birth of Christianity during which days the blood of martyred Christians must soak the earth as sacrifice. Such will be our consolation. We need to continue to live for our country by living for our God.

Any great country will inevitably become a giant among nations when its very roots, like the olive roots of Gethsemane, which never die, are soaked in the blood of its noble citizens. Just over two hundred years ago, a handful of embattled New England farmers stood defiant before the armed might of the world's greatest empire. What began here in Massachusetts, specifically at Lexington Green and Concord, was a war. The years that followed brought sacrifice, suffering, pain, anguish. For many it brought separation or death. But in the final ordeal, it brought victory and independence. The new Americans knew their God, they understood themselves, and they knew where they were going. They had a purpose both for God and for country. And so, the United States of America emerged. It was the first of the world's "new nations." It was born of blood and nourished of dreams, ideals, sacrifice, constancy, and patient perseverance. Its roots are indeed sacred!

We Americans today are the beneficiaries of that New Birth into freedom purchased at the Baptism of the Spirit. God descends on a nation upon whom He can depend and trust. Each one of us—the black man, the white man, the Oriental, the red man—every human being, be he or she immigrant or native, must try, once again, to muster new vitality for victorious living, to pledge to one another "our lives, our fortunes, our sacred honor" prayerfully perceived through our own daily encounter with God. If we do so, the blood sacrificed by those first gallant revolutionaries will not have been shed in vain; the anguished moment of their respective destinies—their one moment in life—will be remembered as a redemption for all of us.

The lesson learned during those terrible war years by those new Americans echoes for our own day—namely, that a people apparently in strife, apparently wandering, apparently in search, could rise; ordinary people, sinful, quarreling, selfish at times, could in fact govern themselves. Such achievement incited other human hearts living across the ocean. The spark of this torch of liberty lighted a new pathway for millions and millions of emigrants. Countless others, for multiple personal reasons, voyaged the vast oceans to join in that experience. They were hopeful. The promise was there.

A hundred years after the Revolution, this nation struggled within itself. God permitted it to experience inner healing from its greed, social injustice, slavery, lust for materialism. God will not leave a nation called by Him to dwell in its own infestation. He will come with countless visitations to arouse the land to its original vocation. Destinies are indeed very particular, very distinctive. We may physically be free to refuse; but morally we will need to answer for our denial. The Civil War was a cruel bloody battle to preserve that dream and share it with the most excluded of people. In our own times, we have witnessed multitudinous sons and daughters who themselves have given their blood and their spirit. Their life's sacrifice has kept America high and noble, radiating a glow to people everywhere.

Today—apparently more than ever before—we are called upon to examine our own responsibility for the promise of liberty and justice not only for ourselves, but also for those to whom the torch of the Statue of Liberty is raised. You and I are the offspring of immigrants who had THE DREAM. Like those immigrants from whose dreams and sacrifices we were born, we must try to ratify the sacred commitment to self-government and to liberty and justice for all. And this we must demonstrate in the actions of our lives. Perhaps the meaning of their sacrifices is found precisely in our manner of response to the contemporary hard challenges of human existence: challenges in the insanity of the arms race, the cruelty of worldwide economic priorities, the bleaker specter of mass starvation confronting millions of people in the world. Perhaps, like our ancestors, we can find the responsibility of our own moment, seek our own courage to be faithful to the past and open to the future. Maybe we can help one another, letting no brother be orphaned, letting no man or woman remain a stranger, leaving nobody with unheard cries for bread, justice, release from oppression.

Then, as the black immigrant poet, Langston Hughes, put it, we can "hold fast to dreams, for if dreams die, life is a broken winged bird that cannot fly."

30.
Our Nation: A Nation of Immigrants, a Nation of Patriotism

IMMIGRANTS

America is a nation of immigrants. The force and virtue that holds her together as a mighty nation is patriotism. Over fifty million immigrants have arrived in this country since its birth through the American revolution in 1776.

Why did these numerous people come? Why should these different nationalities leave their own lands, voyaging across unknown waters into strange territories? Why should men, women, and children willingly accept and endure unforeseen hardships? They came primarily for greater economic opportunity than they had in their native lands; others came for political freedom; and still others ventured to the new territory seeking religious liberty. Each one of us—you and I—comes from the stock of immigrants with out parents, grandparents, great-grandparents, or even beyond.

Between 1820 and 1930, the American shores smiled welcomingly to just about 60 percent of the world's immigrants. Our books of sociology list that approximately 23.5 million entered the American territory. Where did they come from? Our various cultures and ethnic groups clearly demonstrate that most of the immigrants came from countries in both southern and eastern Europe. Some were Russian, some Polish, others Italian, Irish, and Greek. Still many others came from Japan and China.

Following these first immigrants, many Jewish people also came. As young merchants or impoverished artisans, they brought their talents and their skills. They sought employment; and through their industrial dexterity, they placed their mark of heritage in the founding and building of a new nation.

When a person is in desperate need, and has exhausted all tolerance, whatever nostalgia he may have for "the old ways" is counteracted by the hope for new dreams. Though leaving their native homelands, family and friends, most emigrants believed that no matter how difficult and hard their exit was their sacrifices would be rewarded. Anything would be an improvement over past hardships.

We contemporary Americans need to be inspired by the heroic feats of those who came before us. Can you imagine the emotional strain on them of leaving behind their roots, and all that sprang forth from such roots? They had to face weeks of investigation, not knowing what to bring, and to travel on rough seas, most probably in the ship's steerage compartment. Can you imagine their expectant hope upon arrival as they were greeted by Lady Liberty?

New beginnings are always adventurous, as they are daring. And those who came to America—until the turn of the century—were mostly young men. Many of them, like my own grandfather, left their parents or even their young wives and children behind them as they themselves wandered into the new land, pursuing the best opportunities possible. By the turn of the century, many women had emigrated as well.

But new beginnings bring their struggles; and the struggles of our forefathers—who left us the indelible mark of faith, inspiration, and hope through struggle—were no different. There was the tenement life, especially in large cities such as New York, the crowded apartment dwellings, the struggle with avaricious and greedy landlords who sought to squeeze greater profits from limited space. Houses were so close to one another, lighting and ventilation were inadequate—it proved an ordeal. Furthermore, the environment was depressing. The streets often smelled with foul odors from food carts, fish markets, or from the summer heat.

Equally pathetic then—as now—were the unjust relations between employers and immigrant labor, exploitation and underground immoral activities. But man will not remain repressed or suppressed. He must summon the inner resources of his human dignity to surmount such unfairness. And that is what the immigrants did. They came to these American shores to be free—free to be.

Because the immigrant was steeped in the dignity of his own person, he would not retaliate and revolt against a people enslaved to irrational passions. But with tact, with foresight, with patience, patience, and more patience—and in that order—he pursued education as the healthy path to Americanization. Sound education according to the American way of life would necessarily offer the immigrant a better economic opportunity.

Citizenship, therefore, would follow upon the efforts of hard work, perseverance, individualism, and patriotism. With this, our immigrant forefathers made themselves a home in America.

PATRIOTISM

Emma Lazarus in her memorable "The New Colossus," inscribed on the Statue of Liberty, describes the innermost sensitivities, the profound heartbeat of the immigrants who found America their home. She writes:

> Give me your tired, your poor,
> Your huddled masses yearning to breathe free,
> The wretched refuse of your teeming shore,
> Send these, the homeless, tempest-tossed to me,
> I lift my lamp beside the golden door.

To the immigrant, these are *treasured verses.* They reflect and signify our flag, and the patriotism it symbolizes. To such an Americanized immigrant, the American flag means all that the fathers meant in the revolutionary war—it means all that the Declaration of Independence meant—it means all that the Constitution of a people, organizing for justice, for liberty, and for happiness meant.

The demands of patriotism—in Jesus' line of thought—clarify the true order of creation: God, man, nation. Nation must protect and defend man in all his human natural right; man, in turn, necessarily must respect and serve the nation as one who would respect the hand that feeds him. For this reason, each citizen, in conscience, has three particular obligations. A citizen must pay just taxes, must conscientiously use the right to vote, and must render service to country and to state according to his or her ability to give it, whether this means cooperation with neighbors for the public good, accepting the responsibilities of public office, or joining the armed forces in time of just war.

True patriotism, however, does not end there. A man must love his country, but not love it blindly. The same duty that requires him to give support and cooperation to the nation when it is in the right, demands that he make a sincere effort to correct its mistake when his country or state falls into error. The Church at large, therefore, through the long centuries of its existence, has taught that patriotism is the obligation of every individual citizen. It has instructed its children, in all nations of the world, to willingly surrender love, loyalty, and honorable service to their countries. But governments may sometimes act contrary to the law of

God, as when they violate His commandments; they may ask their citizens to place their country's interests before God's interests, they may refuse to recognize the dignity and duties of the human person, or disregard the rights of other people or nations. Only in cases such as these does the Church boldly tell its children that they may not cooperate with the government or obey its commands. The Church must then bring the country back to the practice of justice and charity.

To the Americanized immigrant, the American flag contains American ideas, American history, American feeling—beginning with the colonies and coming down to our time. In its sacred heraldry, in its glorious insignia, it has gathered and stored, chiefly, this supreme idea: Divine Right of liberty in man. Every color means liberty—every thread means liberty—liberty through law and law for liberty. To the honorable Americanized immigrant, the flag of the United States is not a painted rag—it is a whole history. It is the Constitution. It is the government. It is the emblem of the sovereignty of the people. As did the immigrant of old, we of the present day should instinctively throw up our hats, shout wild huzzahs as the old ensign of our republic passes by!

Patriotism is not a duty. It is an honorable privilege. Jesus, the Christ, loved His own native land. The beauties of its hills and lakes, of its fields and trees, were dear to Him. All through the books of the New Testament runs the story of His deep interest in and love for the people of Palestine. Repeatedly, by example as well as by word, He gave His disciples lessons in good citizenship. The Son of God obeyed lawful authority on earth. He used His power, His influence, and His teaching for the good of His country, as well as for the good of its individual citizens. He paid the tax required of Him; and He told the people who gathered around Him that they must render to Caesar the things that were Caesar's and to God the things that were God's. What Jesus taught His native citizens *then* is apropos for us today.

The basic idea of patriotism is actually taking our inner belief from our minds and hearts and transferring it into authentic action by doing for our country all that it can rightly expect from us. And doing it gladly and with a good heart. This is a duty that everyone owes to the land of his birth or to the country of his adoption. It is a debt that each person must pay in the name of justice. This would be national justice.

Love of God and love of country go together as hand in glove. One instinctively flows from the other. Some very prominent saints of the Church have been great patriots. St. Genevieve saved Paris from many catastrophes. St. Joan of Arc saved France. St. Ignatius and St. Francis Xavier fought gallantly in the defense of Spain before they went out to save souls in lands far beyond their own. St. Edward was a wise and good king of England. St. Brigid, queen of Sweden, was one of the most acute, wise, and excellent rulers of Europe.

God's authoritative voice, protecting truth and morals so that these do not become prey to whim and fickle circumstances, is His Church. His Church has to be the sole rule of faith. Outstanding among the Church's voices in recent years are the popes who fearlessly and boldly, like the first Apostles, stand up and are not afraid to speak out on the important issues of citizenship and government, on issues of life and death, war and peace.

Let each citizen, then, in authentic gratitude proclaim to any foreign enemy who comes in the guise of deceit with intent to destroy: "I am an American. Listen to my words, you enemies of God and country. Listen well, for my country is a strong country, and my message is a strong message. I am an American, and I speak for democracy! My ancestors have left their blood on the green of Lexington, in the snows of Valley Forge, on the fields of Gettysburg. They have battled the noble cause of human dignity and freedom. Our American blood has even crimsoned the waters of the River Marne and the forest of Argonne, the beachheads of Salerno and Normandy; it has flowed on Wake Island and Pearl Harbor. My country will live up to its ideals—ideals for which millions have sacrificed their lives. My country is their eternal monument."

31.
The Enemies of a Nation

The enemies of a nation are the foes from within. A little old nun once told me—so very long ago when I was just a young seminarian, age seventeen: "Ralph, remember this always with reference to the Church. More damage has come to the Church *from within* than from without." Is this not universally true? We find this dynamic within family, city, state, country—all of life. We find it to be true in our business affairs. Many times we find it to be that the closest persons to us are the ones who play the part of Brutus. History repeats itself. The point of interest is that one's ultimate downfall flows from the evil that is closest to us: we can be our own greatest enemy.

A nation is no different. It is just on a larger scale. And each nation can affect the rest of the world. A nation is a beautiful creation permitted by God through the needs of its citizens. A nation, just like the chosen city of God, Jerusalem, can be a source of faith and inspiration, of spiritual and material blessings. It can either be one of the world's foremost sacred and loved political powers or it can, like a Saul of old, like a Solomon, like a David, be caught off guard. It can lose its vision; it can decay, disintegrate, die. Though, like many false nations, it may speak of peace, on the other hand, it can become the devil's sword, a tool of destruction. Yes, the enemies of a nation are the foes lurking within seeking to devour.

The enemy of a nation is the enemy of the people; and, as mentioned before, the enemy of the people is the Evil One, Lucifer. He is a fallen angel. All the angels of hell are fallen angels. They are perceived as tempters to evil, and therefore to destruction. Satan, or Lucifer, was once part of the spirit of angelic creation. The Jewish, the Christian, and the Islamic translation of his name is *adversary*. This ugly, former angelic spirit is looked upon as an evil principle conceived as a person.

In Christian theological understanding, this destructive principle of evil was the leader of a proud rebellion, influencing other angels to rebel against God. He was once very close to God: the nearest to the throne of God, it is recorded. Together Satan and his followers as a mighty force fell from God's sight, losing their original call. The higher their original positions, the further they fell in separation. Hell, the product of sin, is the *pain of separation* from the cause of our existence and the purpose of that existence. What a tragedy! To rebel against God was to be cast out from heaven. Still in rebellion, with the added hatred of retaliation against God, Satan goes about to destroy God's greatest masterpiece, man. And so Satan and his followers are seen as tempters of men and nations. They are the source of evil—every evil in the world either directly or indirectly. He may approach mankind or nations camouflaged as something positive and beautiful. But in whatever disguise he comes, that evil thing is the same fallen, though powerful spirit, whether called Lucifer, Satan, Beelzebub, Evil One, or Prince of Darkness.

It is, moreover, a fact testified by Scripture that this Evil One seeks with his followers to *inflict injury on man*. "It was the devil's envy that brought death into the world." (Wisd. 2:24) In his cunning, the Evil One seduced our first parents. Even after the Redemption this Evil One did not relax his efforts. St. Peter, to whom our Lord Jesus angrily and firmly scolded, "Get behind me, Satan," tells us "The devil is prowling around like a roaring lion, looking for someone to eat." (1 Pet. 5:8)

To understand our nation's disturbances, it is necessary to reflect on evil. The evils of our times as in times past rise up from the depths of hell. The enemies of our nation are the magnified sins of individual men, women, and children. Without this understanding there cannot be any healing either on the individual level or on the national and global levels. The evil spirits lead us all into sin, and they do this by inflicting temporal woes upon us.

But, happily, God has given us intelligence, grace, and powers of assistance. One of these powers is that of the Good Angels. These are the guardians of men and nations. It is a revealed truth that the good angels generally assist us in the work of our salvation. St. Paul, in his letter to the Hebrews, states: "The truth is they are all spirits whose work is service, sent to help those who will be the heirs of salvation." (Heb. 1:14) That is consolation! Scripture assures us that the good angels exercise their solicitude for our salvation in diverse ways: (a) they pray for us; (b) they exhort us to do good; and (c) they protect us in body and soul.

Incidentally, it is interesting to know that the angels, being of superior intelligence, can influence our minds in a natural way, that is, by exciting sensible representations in the imagination and thus calling forth good thoughts, just as one person awakens salutary reactions in another by speech or action. Thus they can also influence our will, for the will is outwardly moved by the good presented to it, while only God, the Creator, can determine it intrinsically.

A nation is as good as its people. Any nation that would seek to heal the world must first heal its own hurts and sores, its own afflicted and inflicted wounds. Any nation that would attempt to enter into the lives of other countries must have a wisdom and intelligence not only concerning worldly matters, but coupled with a deep commitment to the Word of God and to the urgency of proclaiming God's message to the world while there is still time. If nations do not heed the "signs of the times," there is serious trouble ahead for our world, for all of us who live in it. The book of Revelation, especially Chapter 6, sounds both a warning and wisdom for troublesome times ahead.

To recap, the enemies of a nation are internal corruption, decay, dissipation—a nation forgetting its creation, its roots, its calling, its destiny! The Word of God describes it as the thunderous galloping hoofbeats of the four horsemen of the Apocalypse. They speed forward, these riders of evil, trodding destructively upon our lives. They follow so spontaneously, so automatically, as the dawn follows the night, as winter follows autumn.

We read about it in Revelation:

"I looked, and there in front of me was a white horse. Its rider carried a bow, and a crown was placed upon his head; he rode out to conquer in many battles and win the war." (6:2)

"This time a red horse rode out. Its rider was given a long sword and the authority to banish peace and bring anarchy to the earth; war and killing broke out everywhere." (6:4)

"When he had broken the third seal, I heard the third Living Being say, 'Come!' And I saw a black horse, with its rider holding a pair of balances in his hand. And a voice from among the four Living Beings said, 'A loaf of bread for $20, or three pounds of barley flour, but there is no olive oil or wine." (6:5, 6)

"And when the fourth seal was broken, I heard the fourth Living Being say, 'Come!' And now I saw a pale horse, and its rider's name was hell. They were given control of one fourth of the earth, to kill with war and famine and disease and wild animals." (6:7, 8)

"And when he broke open the fifth seal, I saw an altar, and underneath it all of those who had been martyred for preaching the Word of God and for being faithful in their witnessing. They called loudly to the Lord and said, 'O Sovereign Lord, holy and true, how long will it be before you judge the people of the earth for what they've done to us? When will you avenge our blood against those living on the earth?' " (6:9, 10) (LB)

What do these four horsemen represent? From whence will come these drastic signs, this false religion, this war, famine, and pestilence? What does the fourth portray to the world about death and the sufferings existing in Hades? As atrocious as they are, are these not another warning voice of God to His children to beware, be on guard, protect themselves, because the enemy does not rest? Realistically, in this day and age, just what are these destructive forces? Where are they dwelling? How do they approach us? What are their schemes and their influences? Watch and pray, warns our Lord. Be vigilant!

32.
To Know the Enemy at the Door

How can one recognize the oncoming but unwelcomed guest of illness except by the initial pain he or she experiences? Martin Israel, in his book *The Pain That Heals* (Crossroad Publishing Company, New York, 1982), points out that it is one of the fundamental contributions of pain to make people wake up to a deeper level of existence. What he adds to this thought is that it has become obvious that the problem of evil in the face of a loving God is not to be solved at a purely intellectual level; it is only by traversing the valley where death casts its long shadow that the sufferer learns basic truths about his or her own condition. Personally, I believe, as I have taught for over a quarter of a century, the value of *redemptive suffering*. Though all suffering is an evil, God through the full atonement of His son, Jesus, on the Cross removes the evil from the suffering, leaving it as an occasion for doing good. Suffering, therefore, in the Christian context is not, and should not be, wasted. It has potential. The intelligent person knows beforehand, at least to the best of his capacity, how to bring the soul into the light that it may know itself, and thereupon protect itself from death.

The first signal of danger is pain. I once read a medical report about a twenty-eight-year-old stenographer named Lucy. She lived in western Canada. Lucy had claimed that throughout all her life she had never felt an ache or pain. She was totally ignorant and innocent of the enemy of sickness and its onslaughts. Just as some people are born deaf or blind, she appeared to have been born without the sense of pain.

But the report continues to describe her as she actually appears. If you were to look at Lucy you wouldn't envy her. Her body is a mass of scars and bruises. The reason is that because she lacks the sense of detecting pain—the warning signs of danger that pain provides—poor Lucy has many times suffered serious accidents such as burns. The only way she realized her affliction was through the sensation of smelling her scorched burning flesh. This was her first indication, her first inkling of injury. Because of this Lucy had to be often hospitalized for countless accidents and infections. Unlike us who can ward off the enemies of sickness and disease, which are constantly at our doors, Lucy became the helpless victim of those human evils that the rest of us avoid because from past experience we have learned that pain is a sign we are in need of medical care.

A person remains vulnerable as long as he or she intends to be totally centered into oneself. Eventually one experiences the foolishness of such isolation. Such a one is the victim of invasion from outer, inimical strengths. It is just like a little child who gears all his first years around his own body. It is also a psychological finding that grown-ups have always grounded their world upon their own bodies as its center; and from it a person circles out to learn about the universe.

Man, moreover, though he discovers himself through the exploration of his body, nevertheless remains many times a stranger to his inner forces, his inner being. Each person is characterized by his outward appearance, his figure, his comportment, his size, face, hands, feet. And though all these outward signs indicate some qualities, some personal powers, they do not present an accurate picture of the true spirit dwelling within.

God loves His world; the Evil One hates it. God blessed His world; the Evil One curses it. God offers healing to His world; the Evil One offers infection. God became our Divine Physician; He offered healing as He Himself the Healer became the Wounded. God's healing love for a nation is the seed for the healing of the world.

The world, in its sad experience of illness that marred its primary innocent state, its "clean slate," sought restoration to its former beauty. But it could not regain it by its own power or merit. God alone could renew, resurrect, restore. He alone could heal. The former state of innocence of the world's first creation cried desperately to its creator to be healed from its sickness of soul. A spiritual darkness swept over the world. And God gave LIGHT again; and He sent that light through His Word. This time a different kind of light. This is true light that enlightens every man, woman, and child who comes into this world of sorrow, anguish, suffering, and pain. That Word continues to speak to us, to warn us, to enlighten us, to guide us.

God's voice comes forth from the heavens loud and clear: "I am the Lord your God; you shall not have strange gods before me." The full text of the First Commandment is found in the book of Exodus 20:2-5: "I am Yahweh your God who brought you out of the land of Egypt, out of the house of slavery. You shall have no gods except me. You shall not make yourself a carved image or any likeness of anything in heaven or on earth beneath or in the waters under the earth. You shall not bow down to them or serve them." (See also Deuteronomy 5:6.)

The Evil One despises praise and honor to the Almighty. He would have mankind deny the truth that God is our Creator, our Supreme Lord and Master. No matter how the Evil One denies this, the fact remains that we are and have everything from God, and we owe everything to Him. Just think of it—suppose God withdrew from us His sustaining power. We all would at once return into nothingness. And so, for this reason, we must acknowledge truth as truth that God is supreme excellence. And we do this by professing our entire subjection to Him and dependence upon Him. We honor Him in a manner befitting a Supreme Being. We worship Him by faith, by hope, by charity, by prayer and adoration. And since God created both our soul and body, since He is the author of society as well as of the individual, each one of us must worship Him not merely internally and privately but also externally and publicly.

The Evil One despises authority. There is power in authority. Like the boy, Jesus, one can grow in wisdom and age through obedience to authority. All great figures of history have exemplified respect for authority. Exodus 20:12 states: "Honor your father and your mother so that you may have a long life in the land that Yahweh your God has given to you." Like the other commandments of God, this fourth one has a double aspect: it commands us to do certain things and forbids us to do others.

On the one hand, it states that children must love, revere, and obey their parents. This commandment comes right after our duty to God, and therefore its importance is profoundly firm. Parents are also bound by this commandment. They, on the other hand, must bring up their children in the knowledge and love of God, educate them, care for their bodily health, watch over the company they keep and the books they read, correct them when necessary, and give them good examples. Ephesians 6:4 counsels well when it speaks to parents: "And parents, never drive your children to resentment but in bringing them up correct them and guide them as the Lord does." And the children, in turn, should have patience with their older parents, support them, and comfort them especially if their understanding fails them. (Ecclus. 3:14, 15)

The Evil One seeks to disrupt. He knows how to stir up dissention among people—on the job, at home, in school, anywhere. His tactic is to stir up our emotions of envy, jealousy, hate, anger, resentment, bitterness. The effects are terrible. Take, for instance, conflict in the workplace. St. Paul's thoughts in his letter to the Colossians offer a sound basis of the Christian doctrine on the relations of employers and employees as well as the labor issue (3:22–25 and 4:1). Social reconstructionists can learn practical success from them. If we would only heed God's ways in love, justice, and peace.

It seems appropriate at this point to reflect on the right-to-life issue. The life of every human is sacred as the creation of God, and it is of infinite value simply because God created each person. RESPECT FOR LIFE as a basic good demands that we do not destroy innocent human life—whether in or out of the womb. It also imposes some duty to preserve life, for example, to eat, to drink, to take ordinary precautions to maintain health. The question under discussion today is the extent of this duty. Is there a limit to this duty? Does one have the right to destroy human life under certain circumstances?

The Evil One hates human life. Anything that upsets the order of God is his objective. He despises human persons who are meant for the eternal heaven from whence he himself fell. The devil never lets our evil look like evil. He causes people to satisfy their inner desires by irrational reasoning. But no person can calmly live in peace with a willfully disturbed conscience—unless such a person succeeds, at least publicly, to "freeze" his soul.

Mercy killing is the ending of suffering and the procuring of painless death by such means as a large dose of drugs or opiates. It has been suggested for the aged, for deformed and misshapen infants, for the hopelessly ill, for the insane, and so forth. Those of you who are young now might some day be old or infirm and fall into the first category. Have you thought of that?

Mercy killing has also been applied to persons suffering from incurable, terminal diseases. The list can become endless. This practice is rampant in our nation. This crime is crying up to the heavens. And the land will suffer more than it is suffering now because of its crimes. Pagan Rome is not far away; it is in our own backyards.

As a young student of theology in the 1950s, I remember reading a newspaper article about the Bollinger baby. Its physicians permitted the baby to die on the plea that it would have grown up deformed. Another case was reported some decades ago in the *Commercial Tribune* of Cin-

cinnati. It said that a physician had done away with several infants on similar pleas. There was also a Nebraska medical man who by means of a hypodermic needle injected drugs into two tramps who were caught underneath a wreck and killed them. It is truly sad that supposedly civilized nations, blessed by the Almighty, should legalize such practice. Where is this to end? Are you and I probably next? Your mother, your father, your own little child? Life is a gift of God. *It is not ours.* It is His.

Mercy killing is *murder.* One may call it by another name such as euthanasia. But that is only a new "sophisticated" medical term for the same *murder.* To kill a fellow mortal in pain, even at his own request and regardless of motive, is against God. And the blood of the victims "cries" to heaven. Heaven *cannot bless* a nation severed from its God by such sophisticated atrocities. "You shall not kill" is a principle of the natural law; it is part of healthy, sound reason. It is a *commandment* of God. It is naturally imbedded in our hearts and consciences. And no pill, no psychiatric skill can remove sin. It has no power to save souls. Only repentance and rededication to God can restore peace of soul and peace of mind. The offense is against God, and only God will deal with it in justice. One must remember that God's justice is just as equal as His mercy. Both will have their moment!

Both abortion and euthanasia are vile attacks on the dignity of man. Every man, woman, and child, at any age in life—no matter how hopeless his or her condition may be—is formed in God's image and likeness, and redeemed by Christ's precious blood. Such people are members of Christ's body. Each person is destined for eternal glory. As long as people are activated by such sublime doctrines as these, abortion, infanticide, or genocide *will never get ahead!* As a matter of fact, the principal exponents of mercy killing today are self-serving materialists, atheists, and infidels. They are people to whom human life is cheap, who consider the person as a mere animal, and who worship at the shrine of pleasure and of the American dollar.

As to capital punishment, it is necessary to follow the truth to its entirety. If God is the Supreme Lord of life, can the Christian Church justify capital punishment? And if in certain instances capital punishment is permissable, then why not euthanasia?

The answer is that to God alone belongs the right over life and death. When the state executes a criminal, it does not mean that the state is usurping Divine Power. To God alone belongs the *full* and *direct* right over human life. But God *can* delegate, and, in fact has delegated, indirect power to civil authority. The killing of a criminal is not *intrinsically evil* except insofar as it is *unjust*. In administering capital punishment the civil rulers are not acting by their own authority, but only as representatives of God wielding His justice on earth. Paul writes to the Romans in 13:1–4: "You must all obey the governing authorities. Since all government comes from God, the civil authorities were appointed by God, and so anyone who resists authority is rebelling against God's decision, and such an act is bound to be punished. Good behavior is not afraid of magistrates; only criminals have anything to fear. If you want to live without being afraid of authority, you must live honestly and authority may even honor you. The state is there to serve God for your benefit. If you break the law, however, you may well have fear: the bearing of the sword has its significance. The authorities are there to serve God: they carry out God's revenge by punishing wrongdoers."

To civil rulers was given the charge to promote the common good of society. Civil authority must provide, by all means at its disposal, for the safety of its citizens and for the public order. It must have the power to efficaciously impede terrible crimes, such as homicide which deprives a person of his earthly life, and can hurl such a one into eternity, the condition of whose soul is known only to God. It could be heaven or hell depending upon how that soul was at that moment of death.

As far back as history can record, the state has used capital punishment. All those who approve capital punishment recognize its infliction upon those crimes considered serious, which are murder and treason. The principle of morality, however, dictates that if the death penalty is out of all proportion to the crime, the state is morally wrong in using it.

By its very nature, capital punishment cannot be corrective. On the other hand, even though punishment can include correction, it is not, however, absolutely necessary. Capital punishment has often failed *as a deterrent*. And it has done so because the fault lies in *the inconsistency of sentencing and the uncertainty of execution* and *not in the very nature of the punishment itself*. There have been very serious crimes that claimed retribution and deterrence as being so imperative that the correction aspect itself had been sacrificed. The law's long delays can often minimize, and even make void, the lesson of correction in all its meaning. Penology claims that punishment to be an effective deterrent should and must be *swift, brief, sure*. A proper sense of civic responsibility must not be squandered by "way beyond a reasonable lapse of time."

Certainly, enough time must be allowed to gather evidence and to give the accused a fair trial. No human being can be condemned to death until after his or her crime has been established by a careful examination according to the due process of law. To permit individuals to give vent to irrational unbridled hatred, exploding itself from the venom of retaliatory unresolved anger, and materializing itself as external violence, is to reduce the lofty dignity of mankind to the dregs of the animal world. And to punish, therefore, a criminal without judicial sentence would be to open a door to countless abuses and excesses.

The state needs to be honest both to God its author and to mankind whom it must serve. The state in its consigned power needs to be humble: it needs to remember that as a state it does possess certain rights, while there are others it does not possess.

THE CHRISTIAN VOICE MUST SPEAK. IT MUST WITNESS LOUD AND CLEAR, WITH TRUTH AND KINDNESS. THE CHRISTIAN VOICE MUST BE HEARD! God will justly judge those who hear, recognize, receive, or reject. The Gospel of the merciful love of a God dying on a cross must be proclaimed afresh—boldly and strong! Scholars of sound ethics and morality have holistically applied and incorporated the Christian Appeal to virtue and not to vice. They have perceived that human behavior has been purified in the alchemy of the Divine. The Christian Voice must strive to let the *healing love* and *mercy* of God supplant the human voice that cries "Vengeance!" Christ, hanging on that Cross, gave pardon to *all* of us. "Father, forgive them; they do not know what they are doing." (Luke 23:34) BUT for the particular instance he heard the repentant cry of the criminal, who in the eleventh hour of his life asked Jesus only for a remembrance. The Lord gave him more than that—much more. Jesus forgave this criminal. Jesus opened for him an eternity of heaven. (cf. Luke 23:42, 43)

The Christian dedication is based on love, hope, and forgiveness. This is healing. We live in an imperfect world. It is peopled by human beings who often are victims of cruelty and injustice. And although society needs to be protected from violence, and to protect human life from unjust assailants, the taking of human life by society must be refocused both ethically and morally, both philosophically and theologically. Otherwise, it is viewed as a return to primitive behavior, which is repugnant to the Christian community.

And so, though the state has the right of capital punishment, it need not exercise the right if it can protect itself from criminals in another way. If the state can prove that it can effectively handle crime without the death penalty, it may be argued that it need not and should not use it.

The purpose of the Christian morality is to be tutor to the state, to aid the state to steer its social course aright; and if need be, to oppose with every bit of its force the state's wrongdoing, if these doings are not in accord with the honor of God and the dignity of man.

So much has been said and written, discussed and argued about methods of destruction in this our modern day. The questions raised on this painful subject, I feel, are best answered in light of the unchangeable simple principles of *preserving life*. One of the most ugly of the devil's tactics for destroying mankind is war.

If a man can use force to protect himself against an unjust attacker or aggressor, so a nation—a moral person—can use forceful means to protect the rights of its citizens, but only under certain circumstances. And that is if public security and public prosperity would be highly endangered. Moral ethics state very clearly that when an individual human being is threatened, he or she can have recourse to civil authority. And so for a nation that is endangered—since it has no higher authority to which to appeal—its final recourse must be war.

But like every other human act (a responsible act of knowledge and will), war is not lawful unless its purpose, its object, and its circumstances are in conformity with the right.

The Christian belief teaches that the waging of war in itself is not unjust. However, certain conditions must be present before a nation may lawfully enter battle:

1. There must be present a good reason, proportionate to the evils that can be foreseen. The reason for the war therefore must be a just cause, as, for example, a grave injustice by one nation to another nation, such as usurping or occupying territory unlawfully, or unjust invasion. These are justifiable reasons for they flow from the principles of justice.

2. The cause(s) must be so grave that they outweigh the evils and the losses of the war.

3. It is only when all peaceful measures are tried and found unsuccessful in remedying the situation that a nation may have recourse to war. All peaceful means, negotiations, mediations, and arbitrations must have been exhausted, leaving war as the final, last resort.

4. The rulers themselves must be morally certain in their own minds and hearts that they are in the right. They must have the right intention.

The warring nation must actually strive to correct the injustice that started the war, and not use the injustice as an excuse for conquering something unlawful. Citizens called to war service should fight for their country, even if they are in doubt concerning the justice of the cause, for the presumption is in favor of the government. Only a defensive war can be justified. However, a nation that takes the initial step to war when it is certain that the enemy is about to attack immediately, can be justifiably considered as waging "a defensive war." The individual citizen must take as his norm the general principle that he is obliged to obey his own rulers *unless* he is sure that what they command is *unjust*. He must go to war if commanded *unless* he has the *sincere conviction* in his conscience that the war is definitely unjust.

5. War must be declared by legitimate authority, as through the U.S. Congress. The reason is that war is an act of the nation; and only the authority representing that nation can declare a state of war.

6. The war must be conducted by lawful methods. All unjust means must be avoided, because they are forbidden by God's *natural law* (they are against reason, as, for example, an attack on the civilian population). Or it may be against the *positive* law (as, for example, in World War I the use of poisonous gas as an instrument to defeat). On the other hand, however, if one belligerent violates a statute of positive law, then the other nation is free to do the same. For this reason there are international laws. The commandments of God and international regulations must retain their force even in the midst of warfare.

We may ask, who is right to wage war? Evidently it is not possible for both parties to be objectively justified in a war. But it is possible that the citizens of both nations are in good faith: that through propaganda and other media of mind influence, they believe that their cause is just. Nonetheless, the waging armies winning the war must offer conditions of peace that are just. All moralists indicate the conditions of a just war to be of absolute necessity.

The Christian faith has always striven to be a forceful exponent and promoter for peace. The Church's message to mankind is that of its founder, Jesus Christ. His message reverberates today as much as in past centuries: *"Pax vobis.* Peace be to you." With these words our Blessed Lord insisted on justice, on human dignity, for human beings, as brothers and sisters in Christ, as members of Christ's Mystical Body. In boldly proclaiming the message of Jesus, without fear, the Church—even if it must once again suffer martyrdom—continues to be the voice of Christ laying down the conditions of a real and permanent peace.

33.
The Power of the Written Word

Many years ago I read a true story entitled "Thoughts." Though it re-counts a frightening event, it speaks to every person who enjoys "the written word." One day, as the story goes, at a Florida high school, a glass exhibition case suddenly burst in biology class. Thirty-five snakes, ten of them venomous cottonmouth moccasins, were sent writhing and wriggling among a group of students! Naturally there was great concern over the poisonous snakes. Fortunately they were all rounded up before they harmed anyone. But the thought of what might have happened is horrifying.

How much concern do we show for the venom endangering our children's *minds?* From the serpents of godlessness, materialism, and evil that poison not only youth but adults? Human minds must be protected from all that is destructive. Every human being should be firmly schooled in the truths upon which America is founded: that our rights come from God and not the state; that the purpose of government is to protect those God-given rights. If people learn these fundamental truths, and know how our Founding Fathers struggled to establish them, they will not easily be infected by those who try to poison their thinking.

We are bombarded with words as never before in history. A century ago it was believed that print would make everyone wise and good, just as food sustains health. But just as food can cause digestive problems, some forms of print can produce intellectual indigestion. What young Johnny or Connie reads now can well determine what manner of man or woman he or she will be . . . doctor . . . lawyer . . . nurse . . . social worker . . . mother . . . father! If he or she comes to know and appre-ciate the kind of reading that is good—especially during critical stages of spiritual and intellectual formation—he or she will be more apt to choose, enjoy, and value what is best in adult life.

God intended that every good human emotion should result in sound, sensitive, and productive action. For example, when the righteous emo-tion of anger emerged from our Lord Jesus, it was aroused against those who bought and sold sheep and cattle in the temple of God. The Master acted vehemently by driving out the merchants with ropes. Scripture tells us He called them a den of thieves. When His heart was moved with compassion and pity, on the other hand, for the multitudes who were like sheep without a shepherd, He fed them by multiplying the loaves and the fishes. Whenever we are aroused by the spirit of God to show mercy to the poor, to the suffering, to the sick, we should allow this feeling to pass into action.

When, however, actions do not follow good emotions, the emotions fall back and make the heart just a little harder than it was before. Just think of how many emotions of fear, anger, love, pity, sadness and joy, sorrow and pain, are aroused by novels, television shows, and articles of all sorts. Many of these emotions never elicit action because the objects on which they are directed are unreal, fictional. Later on, when real objects present themselves, such as the misery of the afflicted, we are already so dulled and jaded that we become incapable of responding. Our hearts have become like springs on old screen doors; they've lost their resiliency.

If you wish to be a man or woman of strong character, develop the powers of the mind, heart, and soul that God has entrusted to you. Outward force comes only from inward strength. One must live by principle, not by emotion or expediency.

Saint Paul, that staunch hero of evangelism to the gentiles, dealt with dangerous salacious literature when he preached at Ephesus. We read in Acts 19:19–20 the results of his wholesome philosophical and theological teaching on the subject: ". . . a number of them who had practiced magic collected their books and made a bonfire of them in public. The value of these was calculated to be fifty thousand silver pieces. In this impressive way the word of the Lord spread more and more widely and successfully."

Since we are united in holy friendship with Jesus, the Evil One knows very well how a breakdown in our ideal way of thinking also brings about the breaking of that union with our Blessed Lord. And the devil acts with this end in view over and over again. It is part of his strategy to attack as many of our Christian ideals as he possibly can. If he can only break through us, he will certainly destroy not only our ideals but also destroy our Christian strength.

If he can tarnish us—especially in the Christian ideal of holy purity— he has little need of expending any further energy upon us. He has accomplished his aim. He has ruined us. He is joyfully satisfied that he took us away from the purposes of our creation, God. This technique on the part of this insidious enemy, Satan, is perhaps most commonly exemplified by the type of reading matter that today's age is being continually exposed to. No matter where we go, literature both good *and* unwholesome is before us. In order that we may avoid harmful literature, we must be able to recognize it, just as Boy Scouts and Girl Scouts are trained to recognize poison ivy or distinguish between edible mushrooms and poisonous toadstools.

What are some of the areas of healthy living that harmful literature can pollute? By the psychological process of influencing, through an appealing manner, the unwholesome product attempts to exploit the lower appetites of men and women. It tries to overwhelm "hungry" emotions with the promise of gratification. For instance, there are some books or magazines that glorify crime or the criminal. This expresses itself as a contempt for law. It influences people to look upon the life of a gangster or a criminal as one of glorious and heroic adventure. This, as you can see, undermines civilization, and civilized people.

Another manner of debauchery in literature is to distort the beautiful emotion of love by excluding commitment. So often sex is projected without love. God, in His wisdom and goodness, has given to men and women wonderfully sacred powers, to be exercised under the Divine Influence as in the sacrament of matrimony. Through the conjugal union God provides in His Divine Love Plan human beings destined for the Kingdom of Heaven and for the continuance of human life upon this earth. These holy and sacred facilities must be kept, and preserved, within the bounds that God has set for them. If not, we become a morally degenerate people. We are no longer able to hope for happiness in this life or in the next. The way in which God's beautiful men and women keep these powers always subject to His holy will and to their own happiness is by keeping their minds and their hearts clean and wholesome. But that is impossible if we keep reading stories, books, and so forth that are not decent and uplifting in value.

Much of our knowledge, whether good or evil, is gained through the splendid faculty of sight. Just as a bad story can send us a message in half an hour, a bad picture is able to offer suggestion to us in the flicker of a moment. This is accomplished by illustrations or descriptions that are either explicitly or implicitly indecent.

Another tool of Satan is misrepresentation of fact. People are easily misled by stories that portray the lives of "ease and luxury" that immoral people often lead. Such a misrepresentation of facts makes people—especially depressed and economically impoverished people—dissatisfied with their own lots. Satan is victorious over young people through this form of misrepresentation of life and its realities. Young people are impressionable and so seldom realize that their real joy of living does not come merely from hours of recreation and idleness but from a valued sense of accomplishment through many long hours, weeks, and years of hard work.

Such writings tout theories and ideas contrary to Christ. They imply that if all men denied the existence of God, and the immortality of the soul, they would be justifying themselves in the practice of free love. Free love leads to pleasure without joy. It increases pain. Free love which produces pain, anguish, and rejection seeks its solace in other avenues of free love without commitment. These include cohabitation or common-law marriages, birth control practices, extramarital affairs, and so forth—culminating in divorce. With these expressions of human depersonalization, humanity would have no religion left in the world.

America, I believe, is the land chosen by God to lead and direct not only itself but a confused and wandering world to a sense of self-consciousness: "Who am I as a nation? As a nation, do I know my God, my Creator and the Source of my abundance?" If I know who I am, and who my source of creation and sustenance is, I cannot help but know how great I am, and where my journey and influence in life be.

Has God ever spoken of this? Has God ever given us guidelines by which we can preserve the wholesomeness of a nation's people? The answer is affirmative. It is in the Lord Jesus Christ. The Galilean of Palestine has demonstratively left His mark. In all ages of time, men and women of all sorts—poets, writers, philosophers, and the like—somehow have all made their appearance, attempting to change the world. They have done so either by revolution or by construction. But no man can ever be compared to Him who has placed His footprints in the sands of time, our Blessed Lord and Master Himself. No man could ever or will ever compare to Him! He was not only a man in human flesh, in human blood, in human thought, but He was as humanly conscious of His humanity as he was conscious of Himself being the second person of God. As Son of the Living God, He would distinguish the spirit of materialism and spiritualism, as He would accentuate the Divine/Spiritual. So men and women would come to know God, Jesus would have to point out the way. He would detach us from things so that we might attain the vast mansions of heaven. Through Jesus mankind would be able to commune with the Heavenly Father; then God, Himself, would do the rest.

Our Lord was very, very clear when He called Satan and his cohorts "false prophets"; and though Our Lord did not proclaim Himself from the Galilean hillsides as one who came in revolution, yet nevertheless, He was a revolutionist against sin and its promoters. His revolution was not to end in destructive depersonalization. His message was the Gospel message of perfection which leads to conversion.

Can we as a people chosen by God, can we as a nation destined to lead, become the promoters of truth and morality? Do we have in our contemporary age men and women, young or old, who will defend the honor of God? Is there anyone ready to lead the way? I believe there is. A group of high school students in Maine have shown what results teenagers can achieve once they take the initiative and lead the way. Rather than merely complain about poor movies, television programs, magazines, comic books, and recordings, they decided not long ago to do something constructive. They appealed to adults to respect their rights to better entertainment and literature. Their demands made many older people sit up and take notice. Better still, they got results. Here is a list of their sensible and urgent requests that they submitted to parents, teachers, motion picture theaters, and newsstand operators:

- Give us decent motion picture and television shows.
- Give us respectable places of amusement.
- Give us a chance to show that we can be responsible, orderly, law-abiding citizens.
- Give us clean, wholesome newsstands and drugstore magazine racks with inspirational stories that can help us in our daily lives, instead of the trash that now blares at us daily.
- Give us magazines and books that encourage us to follow high ideals, instead of those that glorify sex, make of crime and graft a breathtaking adventure, and picture wealth and pleasure as the one and only aim in life.
- Give us your support and example. If through youthful weakness or ignorance we ask to attend these questionable movies or begin to read these questionable magazines, please have the courage to say no to us.

34.
The Raging Thunder of
the Red Horse—Communism

Our nation's forefathers were inspired by the Almighty as they gathered together and in unity of purpose penned God's purpose and preservation of mankind in The Declaration of Independence.

> We hold these truths to be self-evident, that all men are created equal, that they are endowed by their Creator with certain unalienable Rights, that among these are Life, Liberty and the pursuit of Happiness. That to secure these rights, Governments are instituted among men . . . That whenever any Form of Government becomes destructive of these ends, it is the Right of the People to alter or to abolish it.

No greater destructive force exists by the influence of the Evil One than that of The DENIAL OF GOD! The denial of God is both a practice (people living as though there was no God) and a theory (a philosophy or way of thinking that "there is no God"). These theories are sometimes presented in an attractive manner by men of intelligence. We find them in textbooks, in newspapers, in magazines and other periodicals. We observe them also in the classrooms of higher nonsectarian schools and universities. Some deny the truth of God's existence; others teach that we cannot be sure about it; and still others declare that even though a Supreme Being does exist, He is nothing more than a blind impersonal force.

An atheist is one who denies the existence of God. It is difficult to understand how any sensible person could espouse atheism, especially if he or she has reason to observe the world of his environment. An atheist maintains that there was no First Cause of the Universe, that the whole world just began by itself. How can such a person be so "convinced" when the proofs to the contrary are so strong? If you should ever meet or question an atheist, you will find that his or her "proofs" consist of hundreds of denials heaped upon one another to produce one "big denial." Atheism has yet to furnish an explanation of the existence or order of the universe sound enough to eliminate the need for an intelligent First Creator.

No thing in society constitutes so great a danger to all the great rights and obligations as does Militant Atheism. Militant atheists defy God; they seek to eradicate all knowledge and love of Him. Communists substitute the state for God, claim that religion is the opium that keeps the masses in submission. Communism constitutes the most serious threat to those great American liberties that are deeply rooted in the natural law and consequently form an essential part of Christian theology as written in the Bill of Rights and expressed in the preamble to the American Declaration of Independence.

Soviet Russia is not asleep! It rests patiently like a predatory beast, awaiting the right moment to attack. It is the thunder of destruction. It poisons people's minds through the devilish evil of the teaching of atheism.

Soviet Russia sponsored the blasphemous organization called the League of Militant Atheists, whose purpose was to destroy belief in God. It proposed to eradicate the thought of God from the minds of all Russian men, women, and especially from the minds of little children. Today we witness its effects in our schools—as, for example, in efforts to remove private prayer. Such attempts at infiltration exist in both the private and public sectors. And they have existed for a very long time.

It is recorded that small children in Communist classes, as once in Mexico, were taught to chant: "One, two, three!—No God for me!" Did you know that right here in the United States, in 1922, twelve thousand New York children received instructions every Sunday in militant atheism.* There is not a nation in the world that has not been the scene of some atheistic teaching. The reason for this is that although atheism is unreasonable, there are many persons who for prejudiced reasons known only to themselves have willingly blinded themselves to the truth. They really *live as if there were no God!* These are called practical atheists. And to justify their own consciences, they become forces of evil propaganda; they spread the poison of atheism over the whole world—but always with subtlety. They use materialism, agnosticism, pantheism, and denial of the Personhood of God. Although the followers of these philosophies are not

* *A Manual for Pupils Attending Senior High Schools,* compiled by the Confraternity of Christian Doctrine, Archdiocese of St. Paul, Inc., 1942.

always avowed atheists, it cannot be denied that atheism is implied in certain phases of all these systems.

It is really impossible to know exactly the reason why such individuals deny the existence of God. Perhaps it is pride, the deadliest of sins; perhaps it is vanity; perhaps it is more likely a rebellion, a retaliation, against what they think is old-fashioned and difficult; or perhaps it is due to negative environment and evil companionships. Whatever the reason, it is necessarily a distortion of the basic truth that a man needs a god. When he attempts to destroy the true God, then he must invent a god of his own making. And this is idolatry. Like the pagans of old, many people today have set up false gods. Disregarding or denying their eternal destiny and God, they worship worldly goods, science, or the state. The result is chaos. And the true image of man is lost.

In essence the philosophy of communism is to disorientate man by a false adoration. The atheistic Communist purports that men and women have been enslaved by this being called God through religion as well as by private property. They speak of "alienating" from one's true nature. In their logic, they contend that men and women must never allow themselves to become subservient to anyone like God. Capitalism is also an object of their attack because they teach it to be a destroyer of man because it too, like religion, alienates the human being from himself or herself through private property. One should never be subject to an employer, they forcefully proclaim. And for the reason of survival, therefore, in their perverted thinking, religion and private property must be destroyed if man is to be really free. In the lines of this thinking, therefore, you and I, any intelligent person, can perceive the consequences. We would thereupon have in our midst a system of social organization, with a philosophy proclaiming that property and the means of production must be held in common. This is accomplished by *overthrowing* capitalism by means of revolution. There are even more horrendous effects to this philosophical madness. We have already spoken about THE THUNDEROUS HOOFBEATS OF THE RED HORSEMAN OF THE APOCALYPSE—SWORD IN HAND, AUTHORITY TO BANISH PEACE, BRINGING ANARCHY TO THE EARTH, WAR KILLING, DEATH EVERYWHERE.

Shall we be duped, deceived, fooled, deluded, by this devilish strangling of atheistic totalitarianism? Shall the land sleep lethargically in its own pretentious security? The Evil One is never at rest! The Evil One has his own goals; he has his own influences. He battles frantically like a dying beast being crushed by the heel of the Woman's Seed, the Immaculate Mary and her Divine Son, Jesus Christ! If you wonderful people, in love with God, humanity, and yourself, would only but stop and pray, stop and use your God-given gifts of understanding and wisdom, and perceive this enemy's quest, the fruits of evil will have no foothold!

Every human heart desires peace. Peace is a natural condition. Everyone longs for *tranquility* and *order*. And in spite of every attack against this tranquility, people from the very depths of their beings ardently muster fighting strength to preserve peace.

The spirit of the totalitarian, of the atheistic Communists, offers NO PEACE—only a false order initiated and controlled for their own quests. Within their own territory, their propaganda is talking war against any nation that opposes their own unnatural philosophy. To a world that perceives their motives, the atheistic totalitarian governments speak a false peace. They attempt to distract others from their inner motives, thus affording themselves the opportunity for step-by-step entrance into and conquest of another nation, even the whole world!

Authentic peace and tranquility can come only from God. In God's ordinance of creation, society was made and is bound to give to its people that which is the people's due; and the people, in turn, must reciprocate with what is the due of their government. But both—people and state—must give to God what is His due! This and only this is the foundation for tranquility of order!

Do not let totalitarianism deceive you by its false presentations. Before one can free oneself of any demon, one must necessarily identify the illness or disease festering within. KNOW YOUR ENEMY! RECOGNIZE YOUR FOE! GRASP YOUR ENEMY FROM ITS VERY ROOTS! Totalitarian governments such as today's atheistic communism contend that anything they do for their own benefit, even aggressive attack on and occupation of other territories and nations in the world, is legitimate. If anyone, any government, attempts to disclose this erroneous onslaught against the rights of human dignity, such beings are automatic enemies of the Soviet state. Against any force opposing or threatening the Soviet state will definitely wage war so as to protect its own Soviet revolution from anything that opposes it.

This we can see, is an erroneous way of thinking and living, totally contrary to human dignity. It is a form of government in which the state controls all phases of the people's lives. It recognizes only itself as a ruling party and has only one absolute ruler. Force and violence are the weapons by which such totalitarian dictators maintain power and position. Freedom of religion does not exist; and permission to practice religion is granted only to those denominations and ecclesial ministers who cooperate with the government. As to free enterprise there is absolutely no chance. Labor unions, seeking just conditions adequate to human dignity, are outlawed and considered enemies of the government. The government determines the economic policy. All forms of communication and public media are under the absolute protection and manipulation of the regime. The doctrine taught is strictly from the party line; all output must reflect the regime's own doctrine, be preserved, and therefore, approved by it only.

But history shows how such contrary movements necessarily collapse. Their very foundation is not sound; it is not based upon the uniqueness of man's creation; it does injustice to creation. Most all of us have seen or heard about the destruction to humanity wrought by "fly-by-night" regimes such as Nazi Germany, and the fascists in Italy during the years of the 1920s to 1945, and other such governments among us. Others are still attempting to sustain themselves under different names. In essence they are just different flames from the same evil dragon of totalitarianism. They are atheistic in all their aspects. Totalitarianism is built upon a lie; and a lie eventually will be disclosed—it cannot survive itself.

May the American people realize their call: a call to themselves, and a call to share the best of themselves with the world. We cannot reconcile Jesus Christ and war—this is the essence of the matter. This is the challenge that in today's generations should stir the conscience of Christianity. It is our hope that the Christian Church claim as its own greatest moral imperative during the contemporary age, the eradication of evil through atheism, and put the KINGDOM of GOD above nationalism. In so doing, it will call the world to peace!

35.
A Nation Called To Its Knees

Among our most precious rights as Americans is the right to seek God in prayer—as individuals and as *a people*. This is freedom of religion.

The right to practice religion is a supreme dictate of reason. Neither individuals nor the state may sever that intimate and necessary relationship between the soul and its Creator. No man may be hindered from performing his rightful, respectful duties of worship, love, and service to his Creator. Man owes so much to his God—all that he is and all that he has.

As to the conscience: each person has a right to follow conscience. It is only by following conscience that man can perform virtuous actions. These are necessary for him to attain God, his last end and his eternal happiness. Any employer who refuses a man or a woman work because of his or her religion, any state that refuses equal assistance in education because of religion or discriminates against any person just because of religion, is guilty of denying the person a right that is very sacred and inviolable—*the right to religious freedom!*

Anyone acquainted with Russian history—even if only superficially— knows that communism means an absolute denial of religious freedom. Communist phraseology in some of its articles of the Constitution—even those amended—actually relegates religion to the secret domain of the heart and mind, while it legalizes an external persecution of religion. The law does not grant freedom of religious propaganda or public preaching. The law does not grant freedom to religious groups to own or to conduct seminaries for the training of the clergy, or to conduct private schools or private hospitals or private institutions in which religion of any kind is taught or mentioned. But on the other hand, atheists and antireligious groups are given full freedom of expression and propaganda against anything that breathes religion in the Soviet Union.

Many Americans, both Catholic and Protestant, are of the erroneous opinion that one can accept the economic theories of communism while rejecting its atheism. They think one can be Communist and still remain Christian. The Communist Soviet leader, E. Yaroslavsky, in the book entitled *Religion in the USSR* (ed. Robert Conquest, 1968) vehemently denied this type of thinking. He said that a person cannot act correctly, cannot act in an organized manner as a Communist, as a Leninist, if his *brain is poisoned by religion.* We, both as Christians and as Americans, must do all in our power to convince and influence the masses that communism and religion cannot go together. IT IS IMPOSSIBLE TO BE A COMMUNIST, A LENINIST, AND AT THE SAME TIME GO TO A CHURCH!

One very critical manifestation of the communistic rage against religion is in the area of religious education. Communism strives to blot out all religious instruction in a continuous attempt to divert from the sublime mission of a search for all truth. The truth that the universities are permitted to teach is not only colored by strong political propaganda, but is adulterated by real error. This, too, is a violation of an essential human right. For Americans and Christians, each child has the right to be trained and educated both in secular matters and those areas pertaining to the salvation of his or her soul. It is not only a natural right, but a freedom as well.

If truth is right, there is no danger for alteration by any other force of error. The press and free speech influence public opinion. And in the Communist state of Soviet Russia no one is permitted to criticize the government. For this reason there is no freedom of speech or freedom of the press. To oppose is a sign of treason. If any group or individual attempts to charge the dictatorship with tyranny or criticize the politics of the Communist Party, the executive committee that controls the Russian state will immediately commence purging it. Communistic freedom means, therefore, only to agree with communism, thinking what its leaders think, believing what they tell people to believe, and saying only what they want their subjects to say (Article 125 of the Constitution).

This produces soulless beings, indeed, social animals for whom the state represents the entire meaning of their existence. Could you ever think of living like this? Can you imagine yourself not being allowed to use your fundamental rights? Not being able to fight for your justice?

AMERICA, GOD IS CALLING YOU! You have been enriched by the wealth of your hills and by the abundance of your lakes, forests, and rivers. The very veins of your earth are plenished with gold, minerals, copper, silver, and many potent elements, numbering you among first of nations. Before the potencies of the world, YOU, America have become by God's Divine Providence "a living building—stones for God's use in building His house. What's more, you are His holy priests; so come to Him [you who are acceptable to Him because of Jesus Christ] and offer to God those things that please Him." (1 Pet. 2:5)

America, come to Christ, the Son of God. He has proven Himself to be who He is through signs and wonders, especially through His Resurrection and His post-Resurrection appearances. Christ is real; His call and mission were real. You are real; your call and your mission are real. "Come to Christ," come to your God, "he is the living stone, rejected by men but chosen by God and precious to him." (1 Pet. 2:4)

America, United States, come to Christ and be as He was, is, and always will be for His people—CHRIST THE HEALER. Be as He Himself willingly was—A WOUNDED HEALER! With your own sensitivity to growing pains, bring forth the Word of the Creator and cry out to the sleeping nations resting in the death of their own tombs. Cry out to them "to come forth!" Be as the Christ who said in a loud voice to the spiritual man in the sleeping Lazarus, dead in the tomb for four days: "Lazarus, COME FORTH." Be as Christ, and do the same to nations who have lost their star and now voyage aimlessly.

America, if you allow your God to dwell peacefully in your veins, you will be the power of the word in His voice arousing the spiritual man in Lazarus, in the nations, who in turn will awaken their souls to activity. Then, in due time, the nations, resurrected and restored from their seemingly dead bodies, will walk out of the tomb. America, the birth of the nation was under God's direction; and YOU, AMERICA, were destined for WORLD LEADERSHIP!

In the words of the Declaration of Independence, ". . . with a firm reliance on the Protection of Divine Providence, we mutually pledge to each other our Lives, our Fortunes, and our sacred Honor."

Epilogue

With every beginning there is an end; and with every end there is a new beginning. And so the cycle of life goes as our American Indians would dance their ritual: they dance their faith in the symbolic movement of a circle, because all life is as a circle. Sometimes their steps point to the sun, at other times away from the sun. The moral of the American Indian dance is that if we live on and grow older and wiser, we eventually find the real *source of life*. When we do find it, we return to the circle of life from whence we came. Then we learn all truth about the meaning of our life, our soul, our faith. This is the circle of life.

We have made a spiritual pilgrimage together, you and I. The message we have reflected upon still remains to be brought across the lands of this earth. You are to be witnesses to all that is best in life! God does not comfort us to make us comfortable, but to make us bearers of His Comfort. God lifts us up from our own brokenness that we may voyage on and pass on to other troubled hearts some of the helps we obtained during the humble moments of our own weakness. God has not forgotten to be gracious to you and to me. God smiles on us His children, on you His special child, in the stormiest point of your journey.

Let your human brokenness be God's call to you to strive:

STRIVE: to restore Christian values in our materialistic world.

STRIVE: to help the family; children, youth, and adults to become fully human and fully Christian.

STRIVE: to help each human being find God and to love, help, and respect others.

STRIVE: to make every Christian a witness to the Kingdom of God.

STRIVE: to make your nation upright and holy.

Take the pattern of your life and follow it to its fullest. You will find immeasurable rewards! Look up. Always look up! Only then will your soul find rest. There is the voice of the evangelists echoing across the land, sending forth a rainbow of New Hope to every weak human, every broken man, woman, and child. He urges them to rise and live the best they can.

> One night a man had a dream. He dreamed he was walking along the beach with the Lord. Across the sky flashed scenes from his life. For each scene he noticed two sets of footprints in the sand, one belonging to him—the other to the Lord.
>
> When the last scene of his life flashed before him, he looked back at the footprints in the sand. He noticed that many times along the path of his life there was only one set of footprints. He also noticed that it happened to be at the very lowest and saddest times of his life.
>
> This bothered him and he questioned the Lord about it. "Lord, you said that once I decided to follow you, you would walk with me all the way, but I have noticed that during the most troublesome times in my life there is only one set of footprints. I don't understand why in times when I needed you most you would leave me."
>
> The Lord replied, "My precious, precious child, I love you and would never leave you during your times of trials and suffering. When you see only one set of footprints, it was then that I carried you."
>
> "Footprints in the Sand"